HISTORY:
THE HOME MOVIE

HISTORY:
THE HOME MOVIE

Craig Raine

PENGUIN BOOKS

PENGUIN BOOKS

Published by the Penguin Group
Penguin Books Ltd, 27 Wrights Lane, London w8 5tz, England
Penguin Books USA Inc., 375 Hudson Street, New York, New York 10014, USA
Penguin Books Australia Ltd, Ringwood, Victoria, Australia
Penguin Books Canada Ltd, 10 Alcorn Avenue, Toronto, Ontario, Canada m4v 3b2
Penguin Books (NZ) Ltd, 182–190 Wairau Road, Auckland 10, New Zealand

Penguin Books Ltd, Registered Offices: Harmondsworth, Middlesex, England

First published 1994
1 3 5 7 9 10 8 6 4 2

Filmset by Datix International Limited, Bungay, Suffolk
Printed in England by Clays Ltd, St Ives plc
Set in 10.75/14.25 pt Monophoto Janson

Contents

Prologue 1

1905: A Dacha by the Black Sea 2

1906: The Victoria Palace 5

1915: The Queen's Own Oxfordshire Hussars 8

1917: Volkhonka, Moscow 13

1917: Garden Square, Oxford 19

1917: Woodstock Road, Oxford 24

1918: The Arbat, Moscow 25

1919: Back from the Front 29

1919: The Comintern, Moscow 36

1919: Victory V's 38

1919: Anti-Semitism at Babiyegorod 41

1920: Oxford Theosophy 43

1921: NEP and Narkomindel 47

1922: *Muscicapidus humanus* (Patent Pending) 51

1922: Mad as a Hatter 54

1924: Lenin Takes a Long Bath 58

1924: Ainsley's Boxing Booth 61

1924: Berlin am Zoo 65

1924: A Suitcase Full of Shit 69

1925: The General Kills Himself 74

Contents

1926: A Short Stretch of Nothing 77

1926: Roniger 79

1926: The Fly-button Machine 88

1928: Hair Shirt 91

1929: *Locum Tenens* 97

1929: One Foot in the Grave 102

1930: Animal Magnetism 106

1930: Sequestra 110

1930: The Final Problem 115

1931: Sideshow 119

1931: Turncoat 124

1931: Asylum 128

1932: French Foreign Lesion 134

1932: By Appointment 139

1932: Suicide 143

1933: Die Viehbremse 147

1934: No Monkey Business 152

1934: Continuous Performance 156

1934: Standard Bread 164

1934: Answer the Telephone 168

1935: Draw that Fuse 172

1935: Hot Air Mail 176

1935: Who was Bismarck? 180

1936: *Du bist wie eine Jude* 186

1936: Matty, the Acem Giant 189

1936: A Bit of Abyssinia in Bath 195

1936: Hold Your Hand Out, You Naughty Boy 200

1937: Black Sheep 203

1937: A Room for Roniger 205

1937: A Prison Visit 208

1937: Arrested for Murder 211

1937: The Golden Bough 215

1937: England versus Germany 219

1938: The Company Car 223

1939: Digging for England 226

1940: Bergen Belsen 230

1940: *Ja bin die Papi's Spoek* 234

1940: Various Preservatives 238

1940: Christmas Day in Bed 241

1941: Mawcarse 247

1941: Professor Dot 250

1941: The Gorbals 253

1941: Fire-watching 258

1941: Blitz 263

1941: Chistopol 267

1942: Trembling 270

1942: Arresting Ike 273

1943: Orel 276

1943: Tram 279

1944: My Poor Fool 282

1945: Learning to Breathe 287

1946: Reunion 290

1947: Novy Mir 293

1948: Mystical Delusional Experience 296

1949: Bedlam 300

1950: Missing the Boat 303

Contents

1951: Yam Yar 306

1954: Case Dismissed 309

1955: Radiation Sickness 313

1959: Roniger Dies 316

1960: False Teeth 318

1966: Mouth Music 321

1971: Constance 324

1974: University Challenge 327

1977: Irony International 328

1982: History Repeats Itself 330

1984: Gemäldegalerie, Dahlem 332

Acknowledgements 335

Pasternak Family Tree

Leonid = Rosalia (Rosa)
Pasternak | Kaufmann
1862–1945 | 1867–1939

Boris (Borya)   Alexander   Josephine   Lydia
1890–1960   (Shura)   (Zhonya)   (Lidotchka,
                  1893–1982   1900–1993   Lida)
                                              1902–89

= Evgenia   = Frederick   = Eliot Raine
  Lourié   Pasternak
  (Zhenya)   (Fedya)
  1899–1965   1880–1975

Evgeny (Zhenya)   Lenchen   Karlchen
1923–   1927–   1930–

    divorce, remarries 1934

= Zinaida
  Neigaus (Zina)
  1894–1966

Leonid
1938–76

Raine Family Tree

Prologue

And me? Secret Police.
Third Department. Cheka.
NKVD. MGB. KGB. ETC.

An alphabet. Of course.
What else but the filth
in a thousand disguises?

1905: *A Dacha by the Black Sea*

Pince-nez like the letter g,
Rosa is seated, upright
at the upright piano,

letting her fingers rummage
for a few slow bars
of Brahms and Schubert

in its open drawer,
before she finds Rachmaninov,
whose head develops

slowly, stroke by stroke,
crew-cut, severe, three-quarter face,
on the easel in the studio.

Another life in oils,
beyond this empty music stand
that little Lidotchka,

insinuated on her mother's lap,
pushes to a parallelogram
while Rosa looks for lice.

'Shura! *Shu*ra! Where is Shura?'
Boris, older, is in the garden,
a bee unnoticed on his arm,

frowning at the naval squadron
far out to sea. The red flag
he's read reports about

is reading black against the sky.
'Shura!' he shouts. 'Shura!' The name
a headache in the dark indoors.

He wants the telescope,
but Shura is busy being a girl,
his cock and balls

between his legs,
reflected in the looking glass
of passe-partout and blackened mercury.

And where am I?
Seeing this son from behind,
arranged like a bulldog.

And Zhonya? Where is she?
Kissing the dacha steps again,
speaking to splinters

who have suffered so much
and will suffer much more,
laying her lips along the grain.

And where am I? Forensic.
Where the turpentine broods.
By a bouquet of brushes.

Lost in the palette's latrine,
turds of fresh pigment
bright from their bolsters.

So many sticky ends.
Leonid, the painter,
wipes his hands on history

and throws it away:
crumpled columns of Cyrillic,
Gapon, banners and petition,

not a word left in line.
Then newsprint stirs and blooms,
as if the letters lived.

1906: *The Victoria Palace*

Buzz. Front of house, the King.
Ich Deal. Bertie. Edward. Tum Tum.
Incognito on the town.

In the second dressing room,
that celebrated male impressionist
who needs no introduction

from the occiput of Africa
to the coccyx of Tierra del Fuego,
Oxford's own Miss Queenie Ray

takes a Leichner No. 7,
nips it like a *papirosa*
and adds a moustache to her 5 and 9.

A tick of black. A mirror tick.
She licks a brush and loads the point
with lilac to outline her lips,

reflects on her reflection,
completes the job with cochineal.
Her mouth begins to kiss itself,

then stops. She tests a smile out.
It vanishes without a trace.
Her hair is patent leather

with pomade, her patent shoes
are coaldust in the cracks,
her suit too tight for pregnancy.

Five minutes, please.
Backstud, bone china dicky,
starched collar points

a pair of piggy ears
soiled slightly pink,
cufflinks, gibus, cane.

She does the tipsy toff
by business with the monocle,
and hiccoughs as a facial tic.

Nothing loud or broad
and far too subtle for an audience
distracted by the King.

Risking her private routine
of the toff taken short,
she turns her back on everyone.

Left hand on hip, she looks
both ways. The right is urgent
but invisible, the elbow

barely moving. Like a violinist.
On their toes, the legs divide.
Her head is down, but thrown back

when a cymbal simmers in the pit.
A shake. A pause. She bobs
her bottom out and buttons up.

The audience are not amused.
She dies the death.
Curtains sweep the stage.

'She took her Bradburys
and buggered off,'
the flyman tells stagedoor.

'The only effing patter
she's effing fit for
is tiny effing feet.

I nearly had a heart attack.
I could see his majesty was shocked.
But beautiful turned out.

I love them trouser creases
up the sides he wears,'
the flyman adds, two ticks before

he comes over all funny
and has to take a seat
until, too late, first-aid arrives.

In bed, she waits for the words:
'he was, exactly like, *her* . . .
the Widow . . . Mrs Collins . . . the Bearded Lady.'

1915: *The Queen's Own Oxfordshire Hussars*

A tackroom in the trenches,
its earthen walls
whitewashed like a camembert.

On his letter-form he writes:
Serg. 197394 Henry Raine.
My dearest Queenie,

Your news about our little Alice
came as a bit of a 'blow'.
Just like that. Diptheoria.

It makes you think.
Try not to brood about her.
I have a helmet for the boys

not a scuttle mind or what
they call a pickle howb,
its a shako. Well they'll see.

Half the regiment
is to be transferred
from A T to a Cycle Corps,

but nothing certain yet.
It would have been her birthday
week after next. I miss you. H.

He turns the shako in his big hands,
solid as a leather motor car.
Mudguards back and front,

a radiator badge, spare wheels
holding the chinstrap double
like a bumper on the peak.

Bags of room in the boot
where it bulges to clasp
the curve of the head.

A present from CENSORED.
Its beauty censored itself
by the field-cover of grey.

Twenty UP saddles 1912
are gathered in a corner
scenting like a beagle pack,

and a Hotchkiss machine-gun
stares out through the slit,
propped on its elbows.

Shoecases, mess-tins, bridles,
leather boots for short Lee-Enfields,
fetlock gaiters, portmouth bits,

webbing, pickets, Webley bullets
blunt as crayon stubs,
water-bottles deaf with felt:

his language, this tongue,
this stable way of life
will be lost in translation,

just as the battle becomes
a pair of scissors on a map.
Instead of a chestnut

kiss-kissing up crumbs
on the palm of his hand,
a bicycle with solid tyres.

So much on his mind.
I miss you means that sometimes
he is stirred by the pleat

at the back of a British Warm:
they call it the Chinese chink
or Widow Twankie's twat.

Silk underwear survives
in the feel of hoar frost
on a blade of grass:

a melting reluctance
that stiffens and stirs
and buckles with blood.

As he comes with closed eyes,
he calls to mind
Instruction for Recruits:

if she'll do it, she's got it,
so when you're missing your missis,
take the wanking spanner out, lad.

Disgust. He tucks away
the tang of bloater paste.
Mucous membrane of a worm.

And now there's work to do.
The horses' respirators
are improvised imperfectly:

nose-bags crackling with hay
like Christmas stockings,
waiting to be watered.

It is better than nothing,
but only just. The mustard
burns the eyes as well,

carving out chancres,
and works on the hooves
like spit in sherbet.

With two misshapen canvas buckets,
he makes for the water-wagon
two trenches away,

as a bombardment begins:
old Bill's Jack Johnsons
and a chorus of minnies.

DiphtheeeeeeeeeriA.
Under everything he hears
the voice of his daughter:

Dad, I can read in my head.
I don't say it out loud.
It's lovely. Watch.

I move my eyes on the words.
That's all that happens.
I think-read the words.

She would have been eight
the week after next. Alice.
DiphtheeeeeeeeeriA.

He risks a look,
a look at no-man's-land.
A rusty can is raising

its hat. The khaki dead
in Phenate-Hexane masks
are fixed, like horse flies

feeding on filth
with a black proboscis
and bulging perspex eyes.

Spilling his water,
he tacks to the tackroom,
re-bandages his left puttee

and paints the horses khaki
for the dawn patrol.
A mummy with embalming blanko.

1917: *Volkhonka, Moscow*

A pair of throbbing woodpeckers
terrify the foggy streets.
Sounds of vodka on ice

say something has begun again.
A tram brakes with a yelp
in its old iron scars

and passengers disembark,
without a word, seeing
the driver drop from his cab.

A dark green grasshopper,
cold in the dank daylight
at the end of Volkhonka.

A thousand kisses on your lips.
Boris puts down his pen,
bored with this bogus letter,

the fifteenth today:
between the lines
space for invisible ink.

Unnecessary now perhaps,
given the gunfire
popping like fat.

Caught in the chemist's shop
at Lesnoy Street, the girls
have run to cousin Fedya's flat,

panting, laughing, tearful,
fighting their skirts
and a stitch up the stairs.

'Lida. Zhonya. Come in, come in.
Sit down. Let me introduce
Irina Dmitrievna, another refugee.'

She smiles and lifts her coffee cup
in silence, then takes a sip
and tucks away her legs,

shedding a pair of Hermès shoes.
The left tips on its side.
'So good of Fyodor Karlovich

to take us in. So generous.'
They keep their coats on
and shyly nod agreement.

Fedya wedges in his monocle,
straightens his coat
and goes to telephone their parents.

'Fedya here. You guessed. Good.
As soon as it's safe. Of course.
God knows. Two or three days at most.'

Together they try to watch
the cautious chess below,
from windows four floors up.

Long motionless hours
and then a man is shot,
running, foreshortened, for cover,

clutching his bowler hat
like someone caught
by a sudden gust sideways.

Firing once, his pistol skitters
across the fan-tailed boulevard,
followed by his hat, hesitant,

tipsy, tottering, out of true.
He is wearing white socks
and only one shoe.

Wind plays with his hair.
Soon there are sixteen dead
dossing in their own dry blood

and every corner is nicked
and notched like a door-edge
used for measuring heights.

Straightaway, electricity fails,
except for odd seconds
when the filaments glow

like someone's final drag
on a cigarette end.
After three days, food is short

but Fedya's kerosene buys kasha
and a screw of salt from neighbours.
In a week, the water runs out

and Irina Dmitrievna lies
in the empty bullet-proof bath,
reading Turgenev: *Smoke*,

then *Fathers and Children*,
then *A Nest of Gentlefolk*,
then *A Month in the Country.*

She is irritable for cigarettes,
complains about the cold
and the crick in her neck,

blaming the horrible draught
from the overflow pipe.
Once, gripped by the giggles,

she burns Griboyedov in the stove,
all five volumes, gleefully.
'You don't mind, Fyodor Karlovich.'

He stands, in need of sleep,
his face somehow uncertain,
blurred by the need to shave.

When shelling starts,
they move to the central stairwell
with all their neighbours:

a forest of candle-stumps,
primus stoves, bedding, pans,
and Zhonya horrified to hear

the thumping of rats
only inches away,
like panic in the plaster.

She comes to prefer the bombardment.
Silence brings the sound
of rifle bolts snacking like dogs

and someone trying keys
in the outside locks,
swearing placidly to himself.

Lydia is too tired to care.
This is her open mouth.
This is her thick saliva.

And this is a direct hit
which brings down the ceiling
and destroys the skylight.

In the dizziness of dust,
Fedya's grey ghost
folds Irina in his arms.

'O Fedya, I'm frightened.'
And Zhonya understands at last.
Revolution happens in her head.

Irina Dmitrievna, another refugee,
Fyodor Karlovich, so generous,
seen as if half naked on a bed.

Navy-blue socks, she thinks.
The milled welt of a Hermès shoe.
Nothing is as it was.

She has seen someone die.
Buildings have subtly changed,
pitted like snow under a tree.

Even the tough bluebottle,
transmitting morse code,
can be cracked

like a chocolate
against the glass
to show its fondant centre.

1917: *Garden Square, Oxford*

The wide wooden rollers
have opened their lips an inch,
eloquent with ectoplasm.

Sheets come out as cardboard,
taking their time to fold,
flannel vests like salted cod.

It is a bad back-end. Nothing
dries outdoors. The clothes-horse
waits with hessian hinges

for Queenie to lay the fire.
Old *Oxford Mails* provide
a pile of paper sticks.

She moistens a corner in her mouth,
then the slack is taken up,
rattling like a blind released.

Thinking of something else,
she knots them into triangles,
her fingers black with printer's ink.

When the door-knocker bangs,
bangs, she wipes her hands
and goes upstairs to answer it.

No one there. Across the road,
the garden square darkly drips,
open now, its railings requisitioned

by that taffy get, Lloyd George.
The pavement empty either way,
she turns again to the house:

at the top of the steps,
she can see the black thread
attached to the knocker,

and senses the culprits
concealed in the night.
Knocky-Nine-Doors. Kids.

She puts the lock on the snib.
Soon her slippers are wet.
But the search is futile,

because now he is here,
waiting, behind the front door,
the hands in his pockets

jumping with blood. His face
is clenched, his body shaken
by laughter or fear or cold.

So at first she isn't afraid.
He is young and obviously ill
or sickening for something.

'What's wrong?' she asks, concerned.
Slowly his mouth tears open,
but he cannot speak. He shakes

his head and shows her the razor.
A nervous moth of light
flits over the ceiling.

Eliot, Norman, Alice, Jimmy:
she thinks of the children asleep,
forgetting that Alice is dead.

So when he points to the stairs,
she takes the lower flight
back down to the basement.

'Is it money you want?'
She reaches the tea caddy down
from the high mantelpiece

and the gas bill behind it
drifts down to the floor.
Two views of Bridlington,

foggy now from fingerprints.
He sorts out the sovereigns,
half-crowns, crowns, tanners and bobs,

sweeping the tea back in the tin.
'It's not tha brass ah wants.
It's thee. Tek yer stuff off.'

The dialect is fake and frightening.
'It's cold,' she counters.
'Can I light the fire first?'

He throws a box of Swan vestas,
left-handed, awkwardly.
His right hand holds the razor,

little finger crooked.
With an open page and the shovel
she blazes the kitchen fire:

sucked in the draught,
the spread of Situations Vacant
trembles like a kite.

He has to rehearse in detail
every 'mucky' thing she has to do,
and how many times, and where.

When she knows what to say,
when all the moves are planned,
she strips to her stockings,

afraid he will be impotent
and dangerous. He mustn't leave her
for the kids to find in the morning.

'Say: use me like a toilet.'
'Use me like a toilet.'
'Say it.' 'I love you.'

She tells him his story
till he comes in her hand
with the smell of bleach.

She does it like domestic chores,
making them both a cup of tea
before the shaving and the sodomy.

'What do they call you?'
He thinks. 'My name, tha means?
You can call uz Mablethorpe.'

Naked at the kitchen tap,
watching the water wash away,
clear, lenient, empty, chaste,

she turns her tired eyes
to Alice standing in the doorway,
eating a Garibaldi biscuit

and scratching her leg.
Sandals, as ever, on the wrong feet.
Then, then, she dissolves in tears.

1917: *Woodstock Road, Oxford*

A pair of sturdy steel-frame spectacles,
complete with quarter-face and nose,
designed to mask disfigurement.

Adjusting the sit,
he catches a whiff of her cunt,
haunting his hands.

One startled cobalt eye
and a petrified plastic cheek.
It might be Ozymandias

but it is 'Mablethorpe', whistling
along the Woodstock Road, unrecognisable.
Swatting his trouser leg with *The Times*.

1918: *The Arbat, Moscow*

Tightly upholstered in tucks
like a boxing glove,
the chaise longue's adjustable rest

holds the weight of his shaven head.
He addresses the ceiling,
excitable, ravenous,

while Boris reflects
on the way a mouth works:
keeping out and consuming,

this versatile valve
for kissing and conversation
a sphincter restlessly red.

'When they knock their brains out,
it's like watching someone vomit
on their hands and knees,

and it sounds the same exactly.
All our plans for poetry
so much pig swill on the grass.

Eh! Just think. And their boots
bang next to your eye. Dubbined,
obese, dull as liquorice.

Listen. If it's winter, well,
there's a Turkish bath of steam
and they use the snow

to clean their rifle stocks.
Borya, I can't be wrong.
All day I can taste the treachery.

It's everywhere. It's in this room.
She says I'm getting paranoid,
but I see it all so clearly.

Bodies. Lugged like paraplegics.
Lolling. Trailing their heels.
And the sound of the spades,

out of puff, like a train.
Did I ever do you my train?'
The great mad head turns,

greyblue, a battered ballbearing,
a question in the eyes.
'No,' Boris says,

although he's heard it before.
It's French, a party piece,
and consists of only one word.

Merde, like a groan, like a gasp,
like a confinement gathering speed,
running the sound into itself,

a syncopated shallow panting
of *Merde. De. Te. Merde. De-te.*
Merde-de-te. Merde-de-te-merde-de-te.

He might be masturbating.
He shakes on the sofa, rigid,
gripped, unable to stop.

'Susik, you're not yourself today.
It's nothing to worry about. I promise.
I promise. It's nothing.'

Boris tiptoes from the room,
careful to leave the door ajar,
and goes to Katya in the kitchen.

'Well?' Thick black eyebrows,
heavy breasts, low, a shred
of smoke slides up a nostril.

She puts the cigarette down
and walks deliberately towards him
until there is perhaps an inch

between his cotton shirt
and the weighted curve of her dress.
'Well, he isn't well. He's ill.

He should really see a doctor.'
She takes his middle finger
in her mouth and sucks.

Merde-de-te-merde-de-te-merde.
His right hand works
the dress between her buttocks.

'He'll get over it,' she says.
But Boris shakes his head.
'No, there's something really wrong.

He gave me this to keep,
in case they come for him.
Don't ask me who "they" are.'

He takes from his jacket
an ordinary exercise book.
'It's nothing really. Notes.

For his thesis, nothing else.
Latin Elegiac Verse:
Functions of the Accusative Case.'

She turns to retrieve her cigarette,
gone dead on the saucer.
'So what do you propose?'

She inhales and wafts out the match.
'Treatment, Katya. Proper treatment.'
She grins, but the light

in her look suddenly warps.
Finally she finds a word
that comes out a question,

'Goodbye?' He nods. And then
her favourite English phrase:
'a fly in every ointment, eh?'

1919: *Back from the Front*

Alice's Adventures in Wonderland.
The golden spine claims
Queenie and the sun.

Her hands are drawn to it.
One shilling and sixpence
expressed as a fraction.

Her lips aim a long breath
and leave a line of dust
in the afternoon air,

straggling yet stationary.
It lingers like magnesium smoke.
And then the little one is shy

and suddenly under her skirt,
like old Stanhope Hicks
the Studio Photographer.

Carefully, Queenie carefully
puts down the book,
as if she could see a child

poised and precious
at a fifth-floor window,
and dare not shout.

Henry. Silent, smiling, handsome,
and framed by the frame
of the sitting-room door.

'Did I give you a shock?'
She is hardly able to nod.
Her eyes are open underwater.

She swings up the child
and puts out her other hand,
letting her fingers

encounter his brass buttons,
the prickle of khaki,
the shape of his face.

'What were you reading?'
A cut on his chin
carries a piece of toilet paper.

He leafs through the story,
stops at a page of pencil marks.
He shows her the scribbled nest.

'Our Alice,' he says,
and all her features refract
in the ripple of grief.

After school, Eliot and Norman
clatter down the kitchen stairs
and into the silence

of Jimmy asleep on the sofa
and the adults absorbed
in the sight of each other.

'Well, just look who's here.
You look like hypnotists, you two.
Don't tell me I've grown.'

'Hello, son.' Eliot submits
to his father's embrace.
For Norman, nothing has changed:

'Dad, is it bad manners or not
to wipe the bottle of pop
when it gets to your turn?'

Together they go to the fields.
A line of willow pollards
have ceased to be themselves,

stony as the faceless emperors
on the Sheldonian wall.
But the cricket square is pale

with care and attention,
adhesive plaster removed.
The patient sight-screens

survive like polar ice-caps,
and at this world's omphalos
one abandoned iron castor.

'Home,' he whispers to Queenie,
watching his youngest lurch
on sturdy statuesque limbs.

He spends the evening
opening cupboards and drawers,
finding the ivory napkin rings,

a set of six, like smokers' teeth,
a tea-strainer's peeling chrome,
Caswell's Kid Reviver,

a tin of Huttonizing Fluid,
the *Book of Common Prayer*
worn away at the corners:

and his desire, yea,
is like to a thick tile of honey,
yet he cannot leave off,

discovering a pile of handkerchiefs
ironed like booklets,
a pair of silver sleeve links,

the metal mincing machine
with Made in England
embossed on the curve of its arm,

a wooden top like a mushroom.
He plays with the carving rests,
the dachshund, the panther, the fox,

resting their lead in his hand,
he opens the meat safe
and closes its pliant zinc,

he touches the oilcloth
tacked to the pantry shelves,
smiles at the smell of Gravina.

He is saving the garden,
wisteria, lupins, red-hot pokers,
for tomorrow morning early.

Tonight he squats to sample
the old sourness
that lives in the sideboard,

and finds the regimental photograph.
She watches while he marks
the faces of the dead.

A trellis of Indian ink
with only ten to twenty soldiers
peering out with wary smiles.

'Enough,' she says, 'enough.
It's late. Time for bed.
You've made a mesh of that.'

Pleased by her pun, she laughs,
and opens the curtains, left
and right, ready for morning.

Upstairs, in the silence,
he has waited too long
to touch the wetness

he has wanted all day.
Desire makes him awkward
like someone in the room

and he is unable to stop her
going out to the bathroom.
He smells his armpits

like a highland dancer.
Mulligatawny, masculine, crude.
She returns in a nightdress,

her face cold and clean,
fingers finishing off her plait,
neat as a flautist.

'I left you water in the jug,'
she says. Her folded clothes
rebuff him from the bathroom chair.

The loofah's shredded wheat,
three coloured flannels
for face, foot and fanny.

In the dark, he clears his throat
like a bolt being drawn
and touches her back. 'Queenie?'

'I warn you, my hands are cold,'
she says, as she turns to him.
And they are. And they are.

She hardly understands herself
why she hates his heart
for sounding so frantic,

like something buried alive.
She cannot tell the truth
because she cannot tell,

preferring this pretext:
'Did you do anyone else?
One of those dirty women?'

'Is that all this is?' he laughs.
''Course not.' He wants her softness
and he cannot stop now. Or now.

Lying awake, she listens,
happy to hear his snore
like a fly in the room.

'You're a good-hearted man,'
she says, and eases him over
onto his side, suddenly easy herself.

1919: *The Comintern, Moscow*

How Leonid's pencil hovers
and settles and hovers again,
until slowly the head

seeps out of the paper,
bearded, bald as an acorn,
chin strained out like a sprinter.

Touching, then taking off,
until V. I. Lenin is there
and there on the page,

brass-rubbed rather than drawn.
And damn that decanter
which is smack in the way,

disguising, distorting
the dead Volodya Ulyanov,
a face Leonid wants to exhume.

The sober three-piece suit,
the neat black boots,
the spare economical voice,

speaking impeccable German,
which spares nothing and no one.
Centrists, pacifists, social patriots:

fingers displayed to fifty delegates
from a conjuror's clenched fist,
and then the empty palm

that stands for Zimmerwald
which has 'outlived its usefulness'.
Lenin bangs the podium,

like a man in pursuit of a fly.
Apart from Albert, alias Eberlein,
whose mandate is against,

conference applauds the motion
and a new International is born.
One abstention: Eberlein.

Leonid is Chicherin's guest,
Georgi from Foreign Affairs,
but I am here on my own account,

disguised as a pencil. Why not?
Consider Trotsky, otherwise Bronstein.
Consider Comrade Stalin,

Osip Vissarionovich Dzhugashvili,
who has listened all day
without understanding a word,

who sits like a goldfish,
blowing smoke-rings
and thinking (in Russian) of sex.

1919: *Victory V's*

A cubist quarry of parmesan cheese,
salad cream, hair tonic, arrowroot,
blunt skewers of barley sugar,

Wild Woodbines in packets of ten,
or loose in fives, sherbet fountains
fused like sticks of dynamite,

butter beans in a turtleneck sack,
a bin of pearl barley, Mansion polish,
Edinburgh rock in pastel shades,

rich tea biscuits, digestives,
custard creams, Lux soap flakes
like stamp hinges, flittering loose,

streaky bacon diced to liquorice allsorts,
a telescope of standard brass weights,
and Roland Gill reckoning up,

reweighing occasional items,
pencilling prices on greaseproof paper,
his breast pocket marked like a powder burn.

On the wooden tray of fancy cakes,
a cream bun grins
like a set of false teeth:

'What can I do for this young man?'
Norman is next in the queue,
reading a list, to which he adds,

half way through, allaying suspicion,
'and, yes, an ounce of chlorodynes'.
In his bedroom, a brickyard

of khaki cornerless lozenges,
each impressed with the maker's name.
He keeps them for the chloroform.

As a way of increasing his stock,
sometimes he sells his warts
to Roland Gill, a farthing for five.

One by one, Gill counts them,
finger touching their texture:
brittle little amaretti biscuits.

Then he wipes the whole hand
with his hand, clenches his fist
and puts it in his trouser pocket.

'Now those warts are mine
because I've paid for them.
They'll be gone by tomorrow.'

Acquiring more means a month
and a pin – to scratch yourself,
to make another wart bleed.

Henry is having his bath,
the tap leprous with condensation,
when Norman knocks at the door.

The coma has almost claimed him:
Henry's 'Who is it?' arrives
as a buzz in the brain,

a memory emptied of meaning
from too long ago.
Between words, a silence

travelling the trek of itself,
only to reach a city of sounds
where it loses the way.

He has eaten his hoard of chlorodyne.
Henry clacks back the bolt
and floats a flannel discreetly,

masking his private parts.
But the boy is beyond all that.
'Dad,' he whispers, 'I'm going numb.'

Amazed as Alice
by how his hand has gone small
at the end of his arm,

by the giant cup and saucer
sunk in the mahogany stand.
For two days, he cannot be woken,

but 'on the third day,
he rose again from the bed',
says Eliot again, pleased with his joke.

1919: *Anti-Semitism at Babiyegorod*

A chinese lantern, the keep net
calms its flicker of light
in the dark Moskvareka.

Sunset touches the tub
of simmering maggots.
The river bank is littered

with tackle at Babiyegorod,
as if some rich kulak
had fallen among thieves.

Rods, reels, scissors,
three kinds of hook,
roundbend, sproat and limerick,

caught in a cork, arranged
like the hairs on a rambutan.
This open pocketbook of flies,

dry flies, wet flies, nymphs,
a practice page of manuscript,
the same illuminated letter

perfected in different inks.
And Shura stabbing the ground
with his penknife

because he is bored, because
they could be boys again
at the end of a day. Because.

'Let's go for a swim.'
Shura's slightly buck teeth
unpeel with pleasure. 'Why not.'

Dark water draws the line
less than half an inch
below their genitals,

rubbery, circumcised, snub,
like a boxer's broken nose,
as they wade out on tiptoe

in the shock of the cold.
Boris and Shura,
dothering like diesels

on a diet of coaldust,
arms outstretched, flapping,
the joke of a duet: 'Brr. Bloody Jews!'

Spent wing mayflies, hackled zulus
give off their queasy brilliance
on the unkillable earth.

1920: *Oxford Theosophy*

Anxious, early, over-dressed,
carpet-beater frogging
on his hired coat,

spotless kid spats
mushroom-plush with kaolin,
Eliot has been asked

to take the seat in the hall
while upstairs is made ready
and chairs are arranged.

The coat's bad breath
of naphthalene he fans away
with his flysheet folded twice.

PHRASES OF THE MOON (it says)
A TALK BY WILLIAM BUTLER YEATS
POET AND THINKER ADMISSION FREE

though a Benares bowl
on the card-table's baize
somehow solicits a fee,

which is given to Eliot,
unasked with good evening,
as people pass to the stairs.

It seems so much the thing,
he has taken ten shillings
before he discovers the gaffe.

The poet will be brief tonight,
his tonsils having been removed
quite recently, not four weeks ago,

by Dr Gogarty in Dublin. O'Racular,
he quoths for two hours straight,
convincing a corner of ceiling,

his notes on a postcard,
each thought announced
with a footman's aplomb:

'and if a man return to life,
is it with the same old wart
upon his nose, the same delight

in tales of theft and murder,
or but with his many-coloured soul
like one unbroken thread?'

Waiting his turn with Yeats,
Eliot sees, angled on the mantelpiece,
the aide-mémoire, and pockets it.

'Lucerne', Eliot's latest work,
evokes a place he's never seen,
not even in a photograph.

Hierophant of the Haemorrhoid Oil,
Yeats dons another pair of specs,
keeping the poem at arm's length.

For Eliot, it is almost sexual,
like a visit to Parson's Pleasure,
the breeze strange on his privates.

'*Lucerne is magical in summer,*
but sometimes the spell is broken —
and the world is never the same,'

Yeats recites to the room. 'No doubt,
you will think me narrow-minded,
and yet I disapprove, disapprove

of a serious concept like magic
being used in this, how shall I say,
somewhat, what, irresponsible sense.'

With this, the specs are doffed.
Two tortoise-shell insects
hang from a thickening hand.

Eliot has a vision of his words
like a pair of feet,
white on the grass, lost without shoes.

At 10 o'clock, his girl, Yvonne,
dazzled, adoring, uncertain,
is waiting by the Bridge of Sighs.

Her love is a burden.
'Christ, you're like my mother, you.
He said it was good. Gave me ten bob.

Oh, and this, as a souvenir.'
The postcard baffles them both:
hooping cowgh mixture for Anne.

Eliot's fingers find the flysheet
still folded in his trouser pocket.
And tear it to pieces. Single-handed.

1921: *NEP and Narkomindel*

His toupee was an open book
but his pallid hands
were guarded on the desk.

They gave nothing away,
not the tiniest gesture,
while his wet lips came and went,

explaining to Lydia
that there were no exit visas
for the family of Pasternak.

There is nothing he can do
and, as if to illustrate,
he takes his right hand

in his left, and shifts it slowly,
like a pointer, heavy, stiff,
to a brass bell by the in-tray.

He tings it carefully,
leaving his hand on the nipple
and curve of the brass.

Before the clerk arrives:
'Germany, you said? Parents and sister?
Yes. Your legs are very beautiful.'

She has been observing his legs.
The desk is without a modesty board.
A caliper clamped to his boot

like the steel stirrup
of a bike's front brake.
Surprised, she looks up.

Has she heard what she heard?
The official shows her
the gap left by a canine.

'Our train is leaving tomorrow.
We must have the visas.
I was told they were ready.'

The beige folder is on the desk,
unopened, left by the clerk.
Again, the missing eye-tooth.

'As you can see for yourself,
there is no record of your application.'
A pause prolongs itself

until, almost primly,
'I must ask you to leave.
People are queueing outside.'

Shocked, she cannot speak.
Will she be able to walk
on her beautiful legs,

out through this ordinary door
and back into Russia for good?
Never to be abroad again?

Hammer and sickle. Forever.
Gilt on red. Cloisonné. Blurred
emblem of the ampersand.

She might be the North Star,
Sarah Bernhardt herself,
making an entrance:

everyone waiting watches the door,
as if the door were God,
as if the door were a loaded gun.

Descending the five flights
of grey stone stairs,
she is stopped by a shout:

it is an old man, breathless,
with trembling sticky brown lips,
who wants her to look at his papers.

'You have a kind face.
They won't look at my papers.
Wrong stamp. Should be a circle.

Not this what's-it triangle.
They gave me the wrong one.
See. So now I don't exist.'

She cannot face his eyes
as he stands there in tears.
He is too old. He trembles too much.

She hands him her handkerchief
and then runs away
down the rest of the stairs.

At home on the Volkhonka,
they are roping the trunks
with their brass epaulettes.

'I will ask Lunacharsky.
Shush. God is good.'
And Leonid unhooks the telephone,

hung in the hall,
an earwig of brass and bakelite.
'There has been a mistake.'

So, next morning the visas arrive,
stabbed all over with stamps,
smashed and smeared like flies.

1922: *Muscicapidus humanus*
(*Patent Pending*)

A caricature of the caricature
all children's bodies are,
this five year old boy

in the scuffed German shako
hangs his massive head
and tries to endure the day.

There is no wind. And nothing moves.
Yet nothing is still. The world
is glycerine in water. Warps.

Thistles burn, a steady blue,
like the new New World Cooker.
The horizon fumes.

'Fucking bloody bugger shite':
his brother is beside himself
because Jimmy won't be banished

but sits on the stile,
a field away, watching the gang.
Jimmy has the look of cod-liver oil

when he takes out his thumb,
clean, moist, pink, seized
by seizures of sorrow.

He is wounded, wounded.
He can hardly walk
a straight line for the grief.

Now they are down in the dell,
being watched through the gorse,
Buck Watson flat on his back

with wide open flies:
his cock is like the handle
of a Gunn & Moore cricket bat

in its red rubber sheath,
an open O tight at the tip.
Which his fingers widen

until, finally, the foreskin
crinkles around the base
of his glistening glans.

Jimmy can half hear the name
of the old Apache Indian chief,
whose moccasin mouth

he saw at the matinée,
wordlessly mouthing words,
that Saturday Queenie played piano

when Mrs Brown had a poorly turn.
What do they mean, Cochise?
And why all the laughter?

Pink as a pear drop
taken out of your mouth
to see just how much is left,

the texture has its attractions.
A tacky glaze
now tickly with flies.

When he jiggles it,
expression leaves his eyes
and a grey stuff comes

out of the end onto the grass,
a tangled chain of lumps
like a Russian word

unsayable with consonants.
'When you've had a milk shake,
how do you make it stiff again?'

Buck Watson smears the sperm
with the sole of his shoe.
'I think about fat people. Watch.'

1922: *Mad as a Hatter*

Straight glass of best,
a bulging leather gleam
like a farmer's legging,

watched to the lips,
thin suds sucked, nebula
breathed to oblivion.

'We had to kiss his boots.
But right at the end
it was anything,

set up in a chicken farm,
a thousand quid,
and half a warehouse

of Sandringham hats . . .'
just to let a tyrant
telephone *The Times.*

Henry is having a pint
with Northcliffe's 'nurse':
note the lump on his eyebrow,

plump as a pullet's egg.
The patient playing poker.
Strong hand. Royal flush.

Henry remembers ex-King Manoel,
overweight outside the Mitre,
sad, posed for the press,

an open fan of creases
at his crotch, dukes up,
his linen lapels

gripped like a kangaroo,
and wearing, *olé*,
sizzle of flashbulbs,

the *Daily Mail* hat.
Tweed. 'The Sandringham.'
A 'free copy' from Northcliffe.

Drab. The mighty fallen.
Henry thinks if only,
of the family fortune,

the famous Paige millions,
lost alive in Chancery
for too long to care.

'The doctors advised fresh air.'
Northcliffe up on the roof:
paisley dressing gown,

pyjamas, hair, words,
all blazed in the wind.
Improving his circulation.

Cause of death: certified
as ulcerative endocarditis
by Horder and Price,

or poisoned Belgian ice-cream
by Lawrence or Leonard Brown,
Northcliffe's altered ego.

'He wasn't himself at the end':
his penis had to be held,
he wouldn't touch it to pee.

Dirty. Something wrong.
Café-au-lait complexion
propped in the pillows,

boasting about Napoleon's hat,
how closely it fitted. Titfer
tried on at Fontainebleau.

'It's all very hush':
his last memo to *The Times*,
a cracked, intoxicated tenor

delivered down the phone,
and typed, and read back,
evenly, without expression.

Bitch. Her Master's Voice
in duplicate, committed
to paper, to the public record:

'Why does Robbins wear
a tall hat in Fleet Street?
Tall hats should be worn

only on special occasions.
He wants to edit the *Mail*
at five thousand a year. Stop.'

Malignant, carnivorous,
even as a vegetable.
Utricularia prehensilis,

praying and preying
on microscopic organisms.
Squeezing. A gutter press.

1924: *Lenin Takes a Long Bath*

A what? A curio, a question,
floating in the formalin
like a dried apricot,

stoned, preserved in syrup,
with five singed hairs,
part of a compote

slowly coming to life.
Cold, Shura gathers his cloak,
its falling, elegant line

broken, bunched up
by his invisible fists,
like a bat in the sling of itself.

Pepa Zbarsky, chemical engineer,
an apron beard over his apron,
observes his colleague,

the mausoleum architect,
from across the lab and smiles:
'Give up? *Pudenda*. Really.

And this thing here's a prick.'
Black as a truffle,
cross section of cinder.

They turn again to Lenin,
tanning the colour of biltong,
deep in his bath of marinade:

fresh oak bark, in solution,
plus lanolin, glycerine,
cod-liver oil, in equal parts.

The vascular system
still flooded with formaldehyde,
his expression is fixed:

pledges of cotton wool
fill out the eyelids,
twine keeps the jaw shut

like a system of pulleys,
in and out, nostril and septum,
up and down, behind the lips.

'I'll make a sop of him,'
Zbarsky says, in English,
ducking the head

which bobs like a ballcock:
'Shakespeare. *Richard the Third.*
Not bad for a chemist.

He'll soon be permanent.
Old ways work best. Evisceration.
Those pharaohs knew about meat.

Keep your aneurysm needles,
your English Swann-Morton handles
for the shape-Z blades. Dyes?

Who needs eosin or saffranine?'
Zbarsky comically simpers,
pursing his mouth to the corpse.

'In less than a month,
he'll be hard as bloody bakelite,
with amyl acetate to stop the moths.'

Shura gathers his cloak
in both hands, holding it closed,
closed as a curtain on stage,

while Zbarsky encores in English:
'Here's fine revolution,
an we had the trick to see't.'

Shura would like to whistle a tune
as proof that Lenin is dead,
but his lips have been sealed.

1924: *Ainsley's Boxing Booth*

The tomcat's long left hook
and a right and a left and a left,
but I dance out of distance,

easily, rest on the ropes,
and leave him licking
his balls like a garlic bulb.

The solar plexus of the drum
a muddy mark, a stipple,
a stain, a penalty spot,

struck by the drumstick,
by the blur of chamois-leather
toffee-apple boxing glove,

collecting a crowd, twos
and threes, while the boys
warm up, jab-jabbing the air.

Old Ainsley, the 'trainer',
is chewing gum like a carp,
his tight right ear

solid as a testicle,
the breathing noisy, thick,
in his bison's broken nose.

'He reminds me, your kid, of oozit,
not the Ghost with a Hammer
in his Hand, er Jimmy Wilde,

not him, not the Rochdale Thunderbolt,
no, he's more nuggety than McAvoy,'
old Ainsley confides,

costively, with puddled eyes,
'it'll come in a minute.
Yes. Him. You know. Nonpareil.

Nonpareil Jack Dempsey.
Middleweight. John Kelly as was.'
Enigma Variations.

Variations on an Original Theme.
Eliot listens, his face
a frown of fake attention.

He takes out a Luxor
from his cigarette case.
Shagreen with silver trim,

it represents debt,
like the brocade of his waistcoat.
His socks are hostages,

have been held by the laundry,
pending payment of bills.
Thank goodness for spats.

A toff with esoteric tastes,
Savory's Sélection Russe
with the unusual mouthpiece,

he has come from Duke Humphrey
and a privately printed,
strictly restricted edition

of Beardsley's *Under the Hill*,
which he is copying out,
regardless of regulations,

in careful copperplate
and word for word, including
Venus and Adolphe the horse,

hot, blunt and heavy
in a damp crook of arm,
vein against vein,

whose come she collects
for a petit déjeuner,
sending the scribe

to the Bodleian bogs
for awkwardly angled
occasional hygienic relief.

From self-abuse to self-defence,
Eliot has come to patronise
his brother and the noble art.

And Norman wins in the third,
by a knock-out, deceptively
dropping his guard,

then lifting his left:
a comic crib of the way
that Eliot farts in the house,

his hand a baton raised,
von Bülow incarnate,
poised on a pause

before the music begins,
when the whiff – fooh –
is conducted allegro away.

Copy cat and cat's paw.
One flyweight opponent
laid out like a corpse.

1924: *Berlin am Zoo*

The lowslung leopard
modelling its expensive coat
for the length of the cage,

the gorilla focusing
his nostrils like binoculars
in their direction,

the Indian elephants
without their dentures,
and Fedya captivated

by his cousin Zhonya,
who cannot make up her mind
to accept or reject

his proposal of marriage.
She is almost in tears.
Marriage seems so intimate.

'Here in Germany, together,
we can make a new life.
All I ask is, think it over.'

In the reptile house,
humidity and a muscular lizard
doing its press-ups,

poised like some Lothario
postponing an orgasm,
flame licking his lips.

'Is it the difference
in age? Does it bother you?'
Fedya finds himself prompted,

conscious of seeing,
fifteen years before her birth,
the Prince of Wales at Marienbad.

She shakes her head.
Brown bewildered eyes
capture his face,

its stereoscopic ugliness:
one hooded eye, the other
clenched like palsy

on its monocle,
toast crumb moustache
above a muscular mouth.

'Do you find me ugly?'
He is thinking of Marx
on the subject of money,

its galvano-chemical power
to buy into beauty.
'You'd get used to me.'

She cannot explain.
'No. You don't understand.'
She wants to weep for the animals.

'It isn't that,' she says,
'I don't care about looks.
Yours or anyone's. Let's have tea.'

Today her period is painful.
The pubic hair is crisp,
a scab of rust, tugged

by the sanitary towel.
Indescribable, the diffidence
she feels, even to herself.

She toys with the tongs,
plays blind man's buff
with sugar cubes. Love.

Outstretched aluminium
somnambulist arms. Reaching.
She has never been properly kissed.

Loops, elastic, bleeding,
the stretch-marked moirette
of her thighs from the famine.

She keeps the secret of herself,
how it is to be her.
Untouchable untouchable.

'Is it because we're cousins?'
Yards away, against the bars,
the lolling mongoloid orang-utan.

'It's good we're cousins,'
she counters, lifting her cup.
'But if I married you,

I'd be someone else.
A different kind of person.'
She means to say

if she were someone else,
she'd marry him. Too late.
She will live with her words.

Like the frozen hunting horn
of Baron Karl Friedrich
Hieronymus von Munchausen

thawing out beside the fire,
after an epic silence
she speaks: 'So I'd better say yes.'

The poor fellow can hardly follow:
'Not unless you love me.'
Her answer is incredulous:

'But I've always loved you.
Always. You're my cousin.
I couldn't marry a stranger.'

Fedya produces the ring,
a d'oyley of diamonds
in a platinum setting,

and closes the box
with a cluck
like a dog catching a fly.

Kissed, she is touched
by the taste of somebody else,
someone whose beauty is plain.

1924: *A Suitcase Full of Shit*

I now possess, he writes,
in forceful gothic script,
a suitcase full of shit.

Brief, a letter of reproach,
unsigned, to Hjalmar Schacht,
leaving the taste of glue

from fifty milliard marks
of postage stamps. Ten of them.
A little quilt of perforations.

The jaundiced five watt bulb
dangles like a suicide
at the end of its flex.

Otto Spek, the concierge,
tilts back his head,
producing a paunch

on the neck of his shirt.
He takes a Josephine Baker
and rogers it briskly

with a match in the rear
before lighting up
and suckling the smoke.

His face is like a snap,
viciously torn into five
or six pieces, then glued

together again any old how,
leaving his expressions
hard to determine, but hard,

in the perpetual dusk
of his caretaker's 'office',
a cupboard under the stairs.

Sixty years of cigars
have packed his nose with hair
like a meerschaum pipe.

He sits, stout as a seal,
smoking, watching, weeping,
waiting to pick up her steps

on the entrance hall stone,
or hear the clish-clash of her hand
on the lift's iron trellis.

The foreign Frau. Frau Pasternak.
With whom he has fallen in love.
Whose first name is Rosa.

Who lives on the fifth floor,
with her beautiful daughters
and that arrogant, elegant husband.

He has spent to the thought
of the buttocks under her dress,
their heavy pink, pulled apart,

white and drained, distorted
where his tufted fingers press.
Sturm und Schmalz.

'Frau Pasternak. Frau Pasternak.'
Her umbrella is inside out
like a rhubarb leaf.

'Let me be of assistance.
What a terrible wind.'
He pirouettes the pleats

and orders them one by one
like a cashier at the bank.
Then the black elastic loop.

The ritual reminds him:
'Something. I show you.'
And he drags out a suitcase,

carried away by his own conversation:
'You see. Inflation. *Notgeld*, eh.
Emergency money. Inflation.

Just like mental arithmetic. Eh?
If there are 3,884 presses
printing off money 24 hours a day

at 177 separate plants (yes)?
and the inflation is running
at 2,000% per day,

how many people are needed?
Answer: 50% to print
what the other 50 have to spend.

Ha ha. Big joke, Frau Pasternak.
Big joke. Something. I show you.
Inflation. A fuck for six eggs.'

Only aware he is urgent,
she fails to understand
even the drift of what he says.

The locks on the suitcase
flip up under his thumbs,
revealing a fortune in notes,

brick after brick after brick
printed on Bielefeld silk
to the value of billions.

Wertlosgeld. With the one word
each bundle is identically marked.
'Worthless, Frau Pasternak,

and I just can't throw it away.'
He is crying openly now,
weeping like a wedge of lemon.

'Silk, best silk, Frau Pasternak.
Like ladies' lingerie,' he chokes,
plunging into the suitcase,

demolished *Notgeld*, brick after brick,
'top quality Bielefeld drawers.
From 1st of December, purely platonic.'

As a spider tiptoes,
quickly she tiptoes away.
Upstairs, she explains to Leonid

that 'Spek is having a breakdown.
Ugh. Those beastly sabre scars.
Purple and ridgy. Like worms.'

1925: *The General Kills Himself*

Every breath, a chair scraped back
across a concrete floor.
Every breath, the screek of a shovel

in cinders, grating the grate.
Every difficult breath
a shirt torn up for bandages.

And when he breathes out,
the click of cartilage
throwing a switch,

and the wisp of a whistle
heard on a crystal set,
the frequency fading.

The General is calmer now.
He keeps a level head,
balanced, between both hands.

As he always does. Chin up.
Like a chap being shaved
by a barber, held by the doze,

which accounts for the nickname,
except that, this evening,
blood has picked out

the detail of knuckle and nails,
like schoolchildren bent
over inkwells, busy with pens.

Norman has run for the doctor,
Jimmy is up in his bedroom,
clipped on the ear and ordered

to 'buzz off this minute'
because the General is here,
incontinent with blood.

He has cut his throat
with a bone-handled kitchen knife
right through the trachea,

only to then change his mind
and dash from door to door,
his head in his hands,

till somebody came. Queenie.
'Musha misha juggler.'
He gargles his words.

'Don't talk. Norman, get Dr Wade.'
He sits on her kitchen chair,
bleeding and swallowing blood,

his breath a deliberate slur
like the slur of the whetstone
he used to sharpen the knife.

Through the blind blinking wound,
the windpipe at work.
Now you see it, now you don't.

It comes and goes
like a glove puppet,
swallowing, swallowing.

Dr Wade is matter of fact,
talking and sewing
while the ambulance waits,

the horse like a surgeon
masked by its nosebag.
'Emergency repairs,' he says,

'a stitch in time',
pulling the stitch
to a pimple of white

before he proceeds to the next.
He whistles a tune.
He tugs and snips.

'You missed the jugular vein.
It's a home' *snip* 'tracheotomy.
Stick to the Gas Board, eh?'

Another tug. Another snip.
Another snatch of *Rigoletto*.
The General was out of tune.

1926: *A Short Stretch of Nothing*

Streaked, freaked, spattered, dribbled,
the henhouse hardens
like a painter's studio.

Jimmy Raine's harem of hens,
pluck-plucking at banjos:
c'est la vie bohème.

A bottle of Empire sherry
wears its tipsy wig
of candle grease askew.

He is absorbed in himself,
pressing his prick
like a spring

back into his body.
Whoops, it buckles
sideways and he begins again

until it dwindles
to a second belly-button.
Quickened, it slowly

extrudes, foreskin crinkled
like the unforced crown
of rhubarb shoots.

With concentrated, moving lips,
he masturbates left-handed
while he reads *Film Fun*,

his mind on Harold Lloyd,
Mack Swain and Fatty Arbuckle,
completely innocent of sex,

even though Colin Dunn
has seen the Doctor's Book
at home, bound in brown paper

on the highest shelf,
and knows the greasy band
you wear to make a baby.

And so this numbness,
like cocaine at the dentist,
comes as a nasty surprise.

His cock is there
as a short stretch of nothing
for maybe a minute,

before it jumps like a frog
in his hand, for plié
after plié, after plié. After plié.

The glaring bantams disapprove.
A row of ginger musquash coats
with padded shoulders.

The cock in plus fours
like Henry his father.
Jimmy fastens his flies.

1926: *Roniger*

The full moon is a mother
feeding her child
with parted lips.

Nervous as a compass needle,
seven months out of Sofia
but still on their way,

they bicker in whispers
across the Austrian border
to Wien and Comrade Koralov,

Georgi Dimitrov, Party HQ,
the *Rabotnischeski Vestnik.*
It is a two day walk

through glass-paper snow
for fifteen adults, six children,
and the motherless baby

in Roniger's arms
that everyone wishes to kill
in case troops are near by.

The bumpy, clenched face
goes off like a siren,
unstopped by his hand

or his crooked little finger
worked between indignant,
trembling gums.

It is a two day trek
through the Neusiedler marshes
from Fertöd to Pamhagen,

with plenty of time to see
the scenery define itself
at dawn like painted flats,

with time to remember
how Orange Guards boarded
the Tirnovo train at Dolni Dabnik

and tore out the beards
of Malinov and Todorov
and other 'bourgeois traitors',

how IMRO beheaded Stamboliski
after they hacked off his hands
for signing the Nish Convention,

how Masha once took him in hand
with a solemn joke,
'this is what we doctors call

the hardening of the arteries',
how he came like a gong,
again and again. Her hips

were thin, flat, curved
as Roniger's hip flask.
Which, inspired, he uses now

to quell the child with kümmel,
so Kochev folds the knife away
and grins his grin of solid steel.

A few kilometres on, the baby
smells sharply of shit; then,
a kilometre more, of nothing.

A crowd of fifty thousand saw
the sacristan, Zadgorski, hang
for planting ecrasite

in Sveta Nedelya Cathedral.
Topped by an earringed gypsy,
with Koev and Marko Fridman.

Roniger was there, to report
the details back to Moscow,
not the way the bodies pirouetted

counter-clockwise, then reversed,
nor how the hangman held his nose
when poor Zadgorski shat himself.

Supposing they were stopped,
what would Roniger say,
asked to identify himself?

The truth? Or lies? Or both?
Pretend to be a Bulgar,
the only definite article?

Or one of the Soviet Red Cross
sent to help repatriate
the thirty thousand Whites

disarmed by Stamboliski
and stranded in Bulgaria?
Or one of Wrangel's Whites?

Or a Bolshevik perhaps,
seconded to the party in Sofia,
but after the bomb

at old Georgiev's funeral,
a refugee from Tsankov's terror . . .
It all depends. Who asks?

He has come a long way,
almost too far to care,
avoiding the Yugoslav border

as obvious and, so, unsafe,
taking the Iskar instead
down to the Danube.

Feinting east, then going west.
Against the current. Good.
Dunai, the Dunav, Dunărea,

Duna, Dunaj, the Donau:
you can bet on the Danube,
like Roniger, to change.

To change, to adapt, to survive.
It is snowing lint again,
like going blind,

then waking in a hospital.
The exhausted children
are hungry and quietly crying.

Roniger lip-reads a mother
telling her staring child,
stupid with cold, eight years old,

he should have died at birth.
The bridge of her nose
is wrinkled like a dog's.

Roniger regrets his skis,
their locust bindings lost,
the ski sticks propped

in the corner of that inn
and left deliberately
like a ballerina on her points.

Children. He couldn't care less.
A burden. He tightens his grip.
A risk. And yet he reconstructs

his route by the children.
Children bathing in the Iskar,
wet and naked on the bank,

cold as grasshoppers.
A toddler's tiny prick
au poivre with sand.

Right at the beginning,
in Drehovica, that girl
arranging coins, carefully,

by colour and size,
one brass, one alloy,
alternate, in a patch of sun

to make them shine.
At Sip Canal, a blond boy
learning sums, his left hand

a laborious trill of counting,
the green tablecloth
askew with concentration.

Another child at Maglavit,
who raised and lowered
a bucket over his head,

testing the altered notes
of the scale he was singing.
And Natasha's son at Buda,

addressed by a policeman
in Magyar, there on the street.
The boy stood his ground

smiling a lion tamer's smile
before he went on his way,
relieved, with a ruffled head.

Feelings? Feelings have left
his feet and fingers.
His features are frozen.

The kids are brilliant alibis,
protective colour
and nothing more to Roniger.

This landscape is like a film
before it starts: bright
and blank, except

for a flickering thread
like a hair in the gate
of a cinematograph camera.

When he almost expects
to start seeing numbers,
a sign appears for Pamhagen.

Only twenty kilometres more.
He tightens on his talisman
and walks. A sign. Of all things.

And the village policeman,
holding his heavy revolver,
clean-shaven, nervous, tongue

trying his cold sore, a boa
of breath coming and going,
as he struggles

to free the safety catch.
So they surrender, like children,
who want to be carried,

lifting their arms,
everyone, except for Roniger.
Then they pick up their bundles.

The inn is like a cuckoo clock
with a cuckoo clock inside it,
and the innkeeper's wife

is taking the baby,
like a cache of explosive,
crooning and crooning.

As she uncovers its face,
Roniger registers
the shock of seeing far, far,

far into the human ear:
a flower's fine mist of hairs
and a stamen of dark gold wax,

which move him to tears,
carried away by what he has carried.
His arms are locked.

Lost in a last embrace
with no one at all.
He cannot even take his jacket off.

Kochev couldn't give a fuck.
Grunting, wordless, he reads
the day before yesterday's paper.

Then: 'Roniger, listen to this.
According to this, it says
that Tsankov has fallen.

And Liaptchev has formed
a democratic government.
Shit. We could all go back

and use the Labour Party
as a front.' Roniger sobs.
'So what's so funny, eh?'

Roniger tries to wipe his eyes.
'Nothing. Just that joke
about the fat Bavarian

who finds a fly in his soup.
He eats it, right, and orders more.
This time, though, no fly.

He calls the waiter and complains:
Herr Ober, wo ist Krebsl? Get it?
I mean, we've come a long way

to get away from Professor Tsankov.
A bit of me, just a bit of me,
would like that bastard still in power.'

1926: *The Fly-button Machine*

Ominous outside the forge,
this quarter hammer loads
the table-top like gravity,

weighing its word,
its vow, a cocktail shaker
cast in solid steel,

left there by Andrew Crawford,
who heads for the bar
and turns his back on everyone,

the big blacksmith's striker,
his waistcoat buckle titchy,
glinting, like a lucky charm.

Unperturbed, Tip Musgrave tells
the one about Lunqvist
on Bank Top Station

to all the avid eyes around,
unbuttoning his shirt
in readiness, and slithering

his broad bright yellow braces
off, with a hiss,
like someone, like anyone,

like Stanley Baldwin getting ready
for bed: 'The same whirr-whirr
that happened with the other chap.

But, whirr, instead of ecstasy,
this agonising pain.
In the end of his dick.

The thing had sewn a button on.'
They have listened
like men waiting to sneeze.

And now their heads jerk back,
dental patients,
teeth black with fillings.

'A florin wasted,'
Tip murmurs to his signet ring,
facetiously frowning at fate.

Two tiny nipples ripen
in the body hair espaliered
up his midriff and across his chest.

'If you don't mind, gentlemen,
I'll keep my hair shirt on,'
he says, and nods at Norman,

who is holding the money,
'Call Crawford over, would you?'
He stands unobstructed, legs apart,

hands clenched in his pockets,
and sets his stomach muscles
jutting like a bank vault door.

Round-shouldered as an ox,
Crawford weighs the hammer, weighs,
takes two preparatory taps,

and then the hammer bounces.
Musgrave totters back.
Two steps, three steps. Stops.

'Blow me down. Life after death.
I thank you, Mr Crawford.
The money, Norman. Thaaankyoh.'

1928: *Hair Shirt*

The primus in chains
like a futurist Andromeda
with a padlock handbag.

The brass fuel cap,
sited in grit, weeping
like a cracked nipple.

Thin saucepans, scoured
the colour of cobwebs.
Worn lino. A communal kitchen,

where a bluebottle goes mad
in the lightswitch
and the lightbulb squints.

'In your honour, poet.'
On the woollen palm
of her fingerless glove,

Maria Judina holds out
an ordinary lemon
like a declaration of love.

Not an old lemon,
with dark, thin peel
tough as oilcloth,

but a thing anointed:
beeswax burnish and blur,
bearing a twig.

Her teeth are bad,
ivory mended with mortar,
but she is beautiful

and Boris has heard
she wears a hair shirt.
Grazing her nipples.

'Just as well mother is dead.
Her knowledge of kitchens
was hazy. Wasn't it, mother?

Don't look so surprised:
she's there by the window,
pulling a face. Aren't you?

Can't bear criticism even now.
When we came here first,
there was a kitchen range.

Before the primus stoves.
She opened the oven and said
she knew what it was for.

Didn't you, mother?
For burning wood, she said.
You burn wood in here.'

Voice a sudden husk,
her gaze a glitter.
The hand, though, is steady,

fingers meting out lapsang,
a trickle of black
straight into teacups,

like withered nails,
an archaeologist's find.
They rust and storm

in the boiling water.
A wheel window
floats in each cup.

'Servants saw to everything,
you see. Shall I play?
Alexander Nicolayevich?'

The piano fills her room,
her bedding underneath,
Scriabin open on the rest.

'Look at the notes.
Scriabin's Sea of Galilee,
clear as a snapshot,

and Christ in the left hand,
still half asleep,
composing and calming the waves.'

She wrings her cold hands,
looks up from her lap,
begins, as if the keyboard

had her by the wrists.
And in the afterwards,
in the deliberate silence

which prolongs itself,
his hand is taken, squeezed.
They press past the piano:

'I want to show you something.
Voilà! A poet's moon.
Describe it for me.'

The full moon prompts,
but he is lost for words,
unable to perform,

until he remembers
a simile seen by his son
from different curtains:

'A brightness, bruised,
like the face of a radish.'
He wants to laugh.

'My son's idea, actually.
He's only five. Zhenya.
His mother was making a salad.

He saw it and showed me.
On the wet chopping board,
a tiny coin of radish.'

The child's sad face,
its brightness also bruised,
making the word: moon.

And Maria's sad face now,
saying, 'A clever boy. Sure.
And handsome, eh? Like his father.'

The tea still on her breath.
Tar. Her compliment hurts.
'Not exactly, no,' he says,

'he suffers from freckles.'
Thickly blotted with bran
on his cheeks and nose.

Boris has complained to Leonid,
pages of purple ink,
that they 'will ruin his life',

and been answered with banter.
He cannot be candid,
but he cannot keep silent.

A few freckles. Are nothing.
Footling. Unless they show
his son is not his son.

He cannot look this fear
full in the face. Which face?
That face of brightness

bruised by distaste
which is badly disguised.
And the fear is founded

on nothing: only a conscience
queasy with lust, like now.
'I would like to kiss you.'

'Of course,' she answers,
this hair-shirted saint.
Of course she answers of course.

Inverted nipples. Empty circles.
Pink as chiropodist's felt
for cushioning corns. Perfect.

And the shirt? A string vest.
Henequen knotted by hand.
Did he expect a garment from GUM?

1929: *Locum Tenens*

Bugs and drugs behind him,
scraped through somehow
at the third attempt,

almost pukka Harley Street
in his short black jacket,
pearl-grey waistcoat,

grey herringbone trousers,
Eliot is *locum tenens*
at Virginia Water, practising

at general practice,
and just about scraping through
with less than a week to go.

Something flat on its back,
dead on the windowsill,
arms folded like Pharaoh.

Phlox and photosynthesis,
a brilliant day,
but his lips are a line.

Dread. He is frightened
to touch the telephone,
foetal, trailing its cord,

a cry on the desk.
Has it come to term,
the threatened pregnancy?

'Virginia Water Three Two . . .'
Listens. Oh hell. It has.
Except for that once

as a student observer,
he's never actually in fact.
But when he did his clinical

he passed the gynie.
And even through fear
he thinks, a second chance

to see a woman's. Oh hell.
The district midwife
has prepared the area.

Her safety razor
has bitten off more
than it can chew.

It gags in the basin.
Below the rash of hot splashes
on the big bald pubic bone,

a fresh gash, engorged,
over-ripe, alluvial,
the inner labia

like chicken livers,
the segmented anus inside
out, a blood orange.

'Her waters have broke,'
says the midwife's mouth,
one tooth tinged with lipstick,

'presentation's normal,
if you'd like to check.
Soon be over now.'

The presentation isn't normal.
When Eliot feels,
it feels occipito-posterior

and therefore trapped.
Or perhaps. But then.
The midwife must know:

the confident crackle
of her rubber gloves
like hot fat, the click

of her starched cuffs
on the dresser, the play
of her muscular forearm

making a sweep, dusted
lengths of terracotta-coloured
rubber piping. 'Push.'

Nature takes its course.
He comes and sees her,
he goes away, he comes again.

'There now, here's doctor.'
He tries pituitrin
to advance the labour,

injecting the air
with a fly-fisher's cast,
and then her taut vagina.

Little sobs of bright blood
at the point of the needle.
A brilliant day:

people are playing tennis,
badly, on a, nearby, court
like bradycardia.

He comes again, he reassures
the husband in the kitchen,
avoiding his eye,

aware of the tap's elastic drop
held in suspense,
butter beans in steep,

bursting their condoms.
He leaves. After 24 hours,
she is too tired to push.

On the pillow, wet hair,
lips the colour of cement.
Eliot calls in the partner.

Occipito-posterior.
Too late to. Save the mother.
Episiotomy. Both hands

whiten on scissors.
Forceps and fingers.
Somehow the foetus

unfolds. Like a telephone.
Eliot answers an arm. Dead.
He wishes he'd never been born,

and asks the partner afterwards:
'Will I be struck off for this?'
'Good God, man.' And, kindly meant,

'It's only a baby. No.
She can soon have some more.'
Now he can afford to feel

for the worn-out face
like a Victorian penny,
suffered, utterly spent,

a ghost which has seen a ghost,
forever vague,
the mind's veronica.

1929: *One Foot in the Grave*

Soft slither of excrements
as she trims the surplus pastry,
dish rotated on her hand.

Egg, bacon and potato pie:
chevron snipped into the top,
brushed with beaten egg and milk.

Queenie, at the kitchen sink,
whittles, lips pursed, brisk,
shavings of raw dough

from her clogged red fingers.
And I am rubbing my hands,
my hands and my head:

an affliction like dermatitis,
the desire to be clean.
The tap is in tears.

Henry runs the pastry rowel
back and forth. A wheelbarrow.
He is trying to speak.

But. There is a difficulty.
A pain in the sinus
dissolving the words.

There is an obstacle:
love he feels as furniture,
as a three-seater sofa

stuck in the stairwell,
its hessian underside on show,
its castors comically prim.

'Is it the boy?' she asks.
He nods. Her image drowns.
'The limp?' He nods again.

'And he's shown you?' He nods.
'And?' And Henry shakes his head.
'You'd best bring him down.'

So Norman sits, eighteen, blank,
with his bags rolled up
like some Masonic ceremony.

His left leg, for no reason,
has shrunk to stone,
a glazed length

of rock salt, warped,
red and ready to weep.
He will never box again.

'You should have said,'
she says, bent down to look,
so he can see her parting

then the parting of her breasts.
'Yes. It needs the oil. A film.
I'll go to Hancock's.'

Over the chemist's counter,
the formula for linmethsal,
kept in the bible, preserved

on a plain postcard. Judicious,
Charlie Hancock like an umpire
deliberating his decision.

'I'll make it up this afternoon':
a green ribbed bottle
tight in brown paper,

filled with compound liniment
of methyl salicylate,
eucalyptus, olive oil,

tight as an onion, carried
through the rain, past blowpipe
tphs of burning leaves

and stumbling paraplegic smoke.
In the dark kitchen,
the reek uncorked, she works

the warmth into his leg:
thick whisky taken, taken,
till her palms are coals.

Will I wear a cripple boot?
Norman wants to ask,
but cannot speak his mind.

Instead, a focused fear,
full of blunt detail:
he can count the laceholes,

he can see the leather,
lengthened by dread
like a hall of mirrors,

sheer as the sides of a ship.
At the back of his brain,
he practises, tries out

the tiring weight
and the toppling walk.
He gets in training.

The kiss of the cork replaced
and then the other business
with the spool of film

exposed deliberately
to what is left of the light,
then burned like flypaper

coiled on the kitchen coals
with whatever was caught.
'This leg will live,' she says,

'I won't let you lose this leg.'
Kicking her old high music hall kick
for emphasis, perhaps.

1930: *Animal Magnetism*

Listen, listen to the water
washing in the gravel pit
like a little girl

wearing her mother's shoes.
The wind at Wiesbaden
finds the wet cusp

of Misha Kroll's eyelid,
exposed by his monocle,
the colour of cooked ham.

He is wearing nothing else,
being proud of his penis
and about to take the plunge:

white feet walking the plunk,
plunk, plink of the planks,
toneless warp of the wood.

Flaps like a beech nut,
his Russian fur hat
weighs on his German clothes.

Naked, no one would know
that he was Stalin's doctor,
or that he'd overseen

the softening of Lenin's brain.
At forty, trim as a boxer,
Uncle Misha in the buff,

part of Lenin's legacy,
the brain surgeon, bathing
before a breakfast of eggs

at Haus Dambachtal,
the small hotel his sister runs.
Like a pair of pliers

a frog flips into space
from the end of the stage.
Uncle Misha is more cautious,

inches down gymnastically,
lowering his legs, slow
as someone paralysed,

then side-strokes away,
his monocle mercury
in the morning light.

At night, he entertains
by hypnotising women guests:
a risqué business

of lifted dresses, garters,
stocking-tops and laughter.
His sister disapproves:

a former pupil of Frau Pasternak,
she prefers the piano,
a light salad of tunes

from Offenbach and Strauss.
Misha lowers the tone.
But Natasha, his niece,

who still remembers Russia,
regards him with awe,
with awe and affection:

he finds her attractive,
and when she recalls
how the firemen's water froze

on the floral carpets
so the children could slide
when the fire was finally out,

Uncle Misha listens,
as once he listened long ago,
avuncular, professional,

to the donkey blare
of her whooping cough.
He lets her light his cigar.

Together they take the train
(tickets tucked in his hatband,
the beech nut in his baggage)

to Berlin, to her parents,
to the Pasternaks (for tea),
to all of Wagner's *Ring*

where the girl is hypnotised
and held by the harnesses
holding the Rhine-maidens aloft,

in which she sees suspended
the survival of her brother
in the TB sanatorium,

his leather corset
correcting a spinal curvature.
She grows into another life.

1930: *Sequestra*

Zhenya switches his front tooth,
hypnotic, woggly, on
and off. On and off,

while his mother, Zhenya,
is cracking cob nuts
between her teeth, doggedly,

with the one-sided grin
of a six year old learning
to wink. The kernels pile up.

But Boris cannot look at them.
At the rust on the nuts,
frail as dirt from a fingernail.

Or Zhenya, or Zhenya: the names
a claustrophobic throb
like the generator downstairs.

Boris has toothache,
toothache like the moon,
her introverted look

of swollen suffering,
his heart in his mouth,
beating and aching.

It all began the day
of Mayakovsky's suicide.
Spring. Outside the windows,

a single magpie perched,
back to the breeze,
its tail turned up

like the corner of rug
beside the iron bed.
The big body lay

under a navy-blue blanket,
all but the head invisible,
and that was turned away:

where the hair was shaved,
a faint blue bruising
like a hard-boiled egg.

Boris was trying to cry
when the sister's voice
climbed up the stairs

clumsily, indignant, arguing
every step of the way,
and entered the room

completely alone,
with her brother's face,
the mouth, the hands, the eyebrows,

and crying out, 'Volodya.'
Seeing the corpse,
she stopped her mouth

III

and every feature spoke
instead, suddenly slurred,
as if they were drunk.

She sat on the bed
and stared up at the ceiling,
silent, smoking, destroyed,

waiting for her face
to heal enough to say hello.
But when the cigarettes

ran out, she gathered up
the stubs, and left,
unrecognisable, without a word.

There was a quotation
from 'The Cloud in Trousers',
something quite appropriate

but unsayable for Boris
whose lower lip was dead
and felt exactly like felt.

A symptom of something,
he thought at the time
but quickly forgot,

being entranced
by the caretaker's entrance,
by the chisel in his boot,

used to chip out putty
from the winter window-frames,
which he carried out

on tiptoe, awkwardly,
back and forth,
till every casement opened.

Suppurative osteomyelitis
leaves the taste
of pig shit in your mouth,

loosens the teeth,
infects the mandible.
And has to be treated.

Boris sits at the table
and lets the hump of the loaf
summon the dentist again,

neckless as a fly,
his antiseptic hands
holding the buzz,

his scalpel, his chisel,
and the chip on his shoulder
and the chip in your mouth,

chipping off the dead bone
until the healthy bone
sweats pinpricks of blood

and the patient faints.
Then the periosteum
is sutured back in place.

The casement hangs
on its hinges. The buzz
of the drill is stopped.

And the ache will not end.
His mouth must be cleansed.
He needs fresh air.

Was it ever real,
his love for Mayakovsky?
Or just a rivalry disguised?

The table stretcher
is worn down to a yoke
by the family's feet.

The boy lounges
between his mother's legs
like a cello.

She tousles his hair.
What plucked at his heart
now throbs in his gums.

She gets on his nerves.
He will get a divorce.
Have Zina in Kiev. Throb.

1930: *The Final Problem*

Glimpse. Visible from Row A,
the welts of her stockings
pulled into widow's peaks

by sturdy suspenders:
Lady Conan Doyle, in black,
takes the tragic stage,

one dizzy Jacob's ladder
just above the knee.
Something to look up to.

Norman is sunk in the depths
of his front row seat
for the best possible view.

Queenie prods her son
with the programme. Slovenly.
Show a little. Over and out.

A crowded Albert Hall,
ten thousand in the audience,
full house for Conan Doyle

six days deceased in Sussex.
George Craze Esq. presides,
his hearing aid

like a lost spermatozoon
having a word in his ear.
To womb do I undress myself?

A single empty chair
is set aside, centre stage:
Sir Arthur's seat.

Will we hear its wicker?
Feeding falsetto gasps,
creaky as a new-born baby?

Is Albert in his consort hall?
Is it one of his haunts?
Victoria, before she died,

her hair like a hen
settled and brooding,
would hold his miniature up

to any interesting sight
he might otherwise miss,
being dead to the world.

Will Albert come through instead?
Ask Mrs Roberts,
the unhappy medium,

hot in her fox furs,
who removes all her rings
and addresses the chair,

announcing Sir Arthur is here.
'But only in spirit,'
Norman whispers to Queenie.

In the café afterwards,
they quarrel. A bandstand
of tiered fancy cakes

is left untouched.
She is furious. He, facetious,
staring through the strainer

like a magnifying glass:
'Elementary, old bean.
Wish-fulfilment, Watson.

Like Holmes's comeback
after the Reichenbach bout.
Alive by popular demand.'

And on the train to Oxford:
'Moriarty's name was James.
Two brothers. One a colonel,

also by the name of James.
The other was a station master.
Just thought you'd like to know.'

His mother is silent.
He has gone too far
and can only go further:

he would like to make peace,
but out of the ether,
singing, his voice is heard,

'Pearly gates. Pork and beans.
Good old pork and beans.'
To the tune of 'Jingle Bells'.

From Reading to Oxford,
all the way, unable to stop.
Pearly gates. Pork and beans.

And in the garden later,
he cannot let it rest:
'Or this bee in rugger kit.

White shorts. Reincarnation.
Conan Doyle turns out for Guy's.
Or did he play for Bart's?'

Angry with himself,
he makes a mark with his heel,
and he buries the bee in the lawn.

Home for the weekend,
almost absently Eliot intervenes:
'Actually, it was Edinburgh.'

1931: *Sideshow*

Jimmy is up in the cradle,
selecting a suitable writer:
an extra small swan,

sable with Kolinsky filling,
or, better, maybe a goose
to flood in the dipper.

He prefers a point to a chisel.
Tasting the chalkline still:
unwaxed linen thread, sourness

snapped between his lips,
leaving guidelines of dust
where the letters will go.

He has the spacing in his head.
In his hand, greatness,
laid on the mahlstick

which flattens its muslin nose
like a miniature pudding
tied up for steaming.

With five years to go
before he is out of his time,
this apprentice at fourteen

can signwrite a sign
better than his boss at fifty:
Tillotson of Tillotson & Son,

stout, ambling, stooped,
nervous of heights,
one afflicted watery eye,

the pores of his nose
pinked by port and lemon,
a baggy polar bear in overalls.

Cold. It is January.
Words are white in the air
as puffs from a pounce-bag.

The skewered rides
are packed away for winter,
for the annual exile:

crowned heads incognito,
all their regalia
stowed under canvas.

The tattooed lady
keeps inside her caravan,
or, shopping, covers up

her skin, floral Axminster
under long kid gloves
like an arm in plaster.

The bearded lady shaves.
Without drawing the curtains,
so that Jimmy has studied

the slap of her breasts,
weighed up their whiteness
swaying like cheese wrings

when she whisks the soap
in her Ladysmith and Mafeking
Commemoration shaving mug.

A pair of reserves
for the Boneless Wonder,
whose sign is Jimmy's job.

The nipples are vague,
without an aureole,
two tenacious drips

of the palest pink whey.
One letter left to do
when Tillotson whispers:

'Churchill. Fuck me pink
with a blue stick of rhubarb.'
The lad is so surprised

he makes a slip on the *r*.
'Always wipe mistakes
back into the letter, boy.'

He reaches for his rag
as Churchill's voice
reaches his ears.

Those squelchy consonants,
confident and carrying:
'They were never out of black,

Brendan, the Victorians.
My nurse, I remember, poor thing:
her relatives died like flies.'

Bracken and Churchill
taking a turn to Battersea,
arm in arm, after sitting all night.

Burly, bowler-hatted,
breathing brandy hard,
Churchill reads the sign aloud,

over tortoise-shell glasses
pulled to the end of his nose.
And laughs. Laughs and leaves.

Turps on the rag. Wisps.
A small snow falls
like freshly grated parmesan.

Later, in the afternoon,
Churchill addresses the House,
disputing the Bill for Trade Disputes:

'What does the Prime Minister
propose to do if defeated again?
The other day I spoke about

his talent for taking tumbles
without any visible hurt.
He falls, but up he comes again,

dishevelled, discommoded,
yet always smiling.
And I remember, as a child,

being taken, many years ago,
to Barnum's Circus by my nurse.
Among the many freaks,

the star attraction,
which I most desired to see,
was billed as the Boneless Wonder.

I pleaded with my nurse,
but urged to no avail.
Another time, she said,

when I was a bigger boy,
for now the spectacle
would shock the system

and demoralise my youthful self.
I have waited in vain
for another time to come,

without ever giving up,
and after fifty years
my patience is rewarded.

These eyes rest at last'
– he points to the Treasury Bench –
'on the Boneless Wonder.'

Bracken, writing to Randolph:
'We're back from the dead.
The Boneless Wonder is immortal.'

1931: *Turncoat*

Words clearing his throat,
lips ajar and out of sync,
jowls sprawling, blood-silted,

on his frayed shirt-collar,
'Pecs' O'Hanlon gives advice,
bronchitic as a bulldog:

'Like pulling purse strings.
Lugs is trouble for a fighter.
Best to lance the ligature and . . .'

Quick, his open hand contracts
into a fist,
as if he'd snatched a fly.

'Turn the record over, Pecs.
You're getting on my wick.
I've got a broken nose already.

Don't sell me a cauliflower ear
because I'm not buying it. OK?
I want to look the way I look.'

Norman's hair is vaselined,
waterproofed like astrakhan,
a shining example.

He massages his right ear,
carefully, with hot milk,
as hot as he can bear.

Attentively, the mirror
chained above the mantelpiece
tilts towards him.

A word in his ear:
bruised, it says, bruised
like a bloody black pudding.

The captious cockerel,
a landlady's man himself,
gives vent in the garden.

Mrs Fulton's other pet,
a big black velvet tom
with a threadbare nose

is out for the count
on her travelling rug,
a reversing MacDonald sett

with alternating colour
in the overcheck. G. B. C.
Blackwatch, the dog-eared cat.

His split-pea eyes alert,
he bats a ball of string
machine-wound to a turban.

Every evening, entertainment.
Records on her Cliftophone.
Norman's nifty quick-step,

Elsie Fulton in his arms
flirtatious, over-forty,
full-figured, solid

as a tailor's dummy.
It couldn't be more innocent:
chaperoned by Mr Fulton,

his melancholy photograph
watching from the mantelpiece;
chaperoned by Pecs,

who winds the box,
folds out its prolix pincer,
and sets Victor Sylvester

hissing, dizzy, on the baize;
also chaperoned
by Elsie Fulton's bosom,

braced between them,
single, abstract, chaste,
unyielding as a bolster.

'If you were the only girl
in the world and I was the only boy',
it couldn't be more innocent,

until she falls,
trying out a fish-tail turn.
Too late, she claws her dress.

Knowledge. They have read
her home-made muslin pants:
Lyle and Tate and Ly.

The record sizzles to a stop.
Out of register,
like a tuppenny blood,

her thin smile betrays
the lavish lipstick
of her cupid's bow. Mercy.

Ease the pain. Nothing drastic.
'Turn it over, Pecs.
Blackwatch, time to go outside.'

1931: *Asylum*

The pock of a pipe removed
by the male sister in charge
and then his smoker's smile

of creosote, tartar, plaque.
A cyst on his cheek
threaded with blood,

he points out the patients,
names and conditions,
while Eliot follows

the bitten bakelite stem
on its intricate journey,
the mouthpiece

an oracular pout
of miniature ebony lips
like an African sculpture:

'That's Cheops Robinson.
You only ever see him
sideways on. Fucking crackers.

For he's a jolly good pharaoh.
You have to laugh.
How-do, Cheops? Eh?'

In the chronic male ward,
iron high-sided cots,
mesh on the high windows,

three horizontal ropes
securing horsehair mattresses
which line the walls,

and, at night,
a dull portwine stain
at the end of the ward,

like a blotch on the retina,
which is only the stove,
clenching, unclenching its red.

Treatment is standard,
secure, behind the times,
nothing occult,

containment, not cure:
paraldehyde and lukewarm baths.
'Applied economics,

you might just say,' he says,
kissing his pipe-stem,
little kisses, keeping it on,

'soaking the rich,
soaking the poor. See?
Restores mental balance.'

Men who are women,
watched by male nurses
in rubber lace-up ankle boots

and dark green rubber aprons,
full-length, a quarter inch thick,
solid as a capsicum,

making movement ungainly.
They could be slaughtermen,
strength in their folded arms,

untouched by the touched
and their tone-deaf noise:
the bleats and the lowing

that live in these throats.
They angle their heads
strangely, listening, vacant,

to what is within,
whatever it is which seems
so angry and so sad.

'They come here, some of them,
with less meat on them
than a jockey's whip.

Now look at them: pregnant,
double-breasted to a man.
Must be the potty meat. Eh?'

When Eliot fails to laugh,
the male sister chuckles
and elaborates: 'Cream crackers.

Brazil nuts. Bisto crazy.
See him? That one, there.
With the periscope up.

He used to be scrum-half
for Pontypridd and Wales.
Evans. Wife trouble.

Before he came here,
capped for Wales he was.
Fly-half. Poor bugger.'

Hairless, heavy, soft,
Evans is troubled by sex,
his sudden hardness

which is hypnotic
for the nude, forgetful mad,
who gather and, gathering,

lose the thread. Of what.
Or why. Do not disperse,
docile at their destination.

Not unlike Eliot,
who has answered an ad
in the *Lancet*. Successfully.

The only applicant
for Assistant Medical Officer
at Derby County Mental Hospital

inspects a safety smock,
kept in case of mutiny,
'if anyone goes really bats'.

Tested for weight,
it tinkles with buckles
like a tambourine.

Four afternoons a week,
Eliot takes the bus
to change his book

at Boots in Derby,
watching the lambs startle
on dirty pipe-cleaner legs,

and one night, towards teatime,
returns to find a charge nurse
lugging Evans from the lake.

Drenched and dead. Eyes open.
Feet bare. Sousing
stabs of water. Sabres.

'It's only three feet deep.
Impossible to drown yourself.
He misbehaved deliberately.

Couldn't have done it
without the safety smock.
Salvation, in a way.

He'd had a bash before.
Wife trouble. This way, see,
he couldn't help himself.'

After supper in his room,
Eliot writes to Mapother,
begging a post at the Maudsley:

'I see no future here.'
Trailing canvas wings
which cross and buckle behind

like a pipistrelle
tying itself in knots,
wrapping things up.

1932: *French Foreign Lesion*

On the unmade iron bed,
a tattered *Petit Vingtième*,
open at the opening episode

of 'Tintin au Pays des Soviets'
by Gabritschevsky's friend,
inscribed 'à Yenia, grâce à lui',

and signed 'Hergé (Georges Remi)'.
The pomegranate head,
Norfolk jacket and plus fours.

The last sardine of lunch:
a crinkling transfer
of molten tin. Tinned.

The lid like a mainspring.
At one end, a tilted
wedge of olive oil

he uses to anoint her lips.
Yenia seems a different person,
somehow not himself today,

a sign around his neck
that says 'Do Not Disturb',
explaining madness

as a psychological sestina,
a tinnitus of thought
like Siegfried's ostinato anvil

and the tintinnabulation,
four pianos and percussion,
of Stravinsky's *Svadba*.

'*Les Noces* it's called.
Bauernhochzeit. The Wedding.
Will you sleep with me?

I suppose I needn't say
there's no one here I want.'
His eyes assume an idiot vacancy.

'You like me, don't you, Lydia?
Maybe not so much as Yura,
but I'm better in bed

than little brother. Really.
Lots of practice. Before all this.
How? With prostitutes, of course.

I picked them up in Munich,
outside a little purse shop.
Königsallee, near the station.

Open late. Quite smart.
You bought a purse inside
and if they took it, then you knew.'

She thinks of Hoch,
financier and Fedya's friend,
favoured by her parents:

the way he offers apricots,
suede lockets, softness
pressed between his fingers,

the way his fingers
feel like gloves,
his breathing bluish lips,

his false ivory teeth,
clenched on a torn cheroot
like a flapping cuff.

A close shave, Hoch.
Shuddering, she suggests a walk.
And now she licks her lips.

Sardines. Sex. Of course.
Sex is the something strange
she has already sensed,

felt like a word
on the tip of her tongue,
insistently absent

like Yenia's moustache,
removed by a nervous barber
deputising for 'Herr Dienstag',

who comes on Tuesdays
from his premises in Schwaben,
but who this week was ill.

No one here can shave himself.
She says, 'I'll think it over.
Now, put some shoes on, please.'

Yenia Gabritschevsky,
exile in exile,
with Saturday stubble,

may leave the grounds
with suitable companions.
Securely, as instructed,

Lydia links their arms,
like lovers almost: only,
she could break his wrist.

Gentleman and gentle man,
artist, sadist, dipterist,
he did his doctorate

on the screwworm fly
which insinuates its eggs
in wounds or any orifice,

both animal and human.
'My thesis advocated
breeding sterile males.

If I ask her nicely,
think she'll suck me off?'
Up the trail towards them,

a frowning girl
follows her arms, bent
as if by the breasts

in her Bavarian blouse,
blonde wickerwork hair
slick at the temples.

Lydia has her answer ready:
'Sssh, on no account.
You haven't even shaved.'

'Weisse Scheisse,' he says,
'you're right. I always forget.
Most improper.' His gaze

unsteadies, quickens, spills.
Tiny stuttering steps
take them to the valley floor.

And so she agrees to sex,
on Saturdays, for six months,
in his private room

which lacks a lock.
The china doorknob wedged
by Yenia's bentwood chair.

Hot, half dressed, oral,
anal, painful, prolonged,
for pity's sake.

Inserting barley sugar
in her cunt, he whispers
'Fräulein Sonnabend' and comes. At last.

1932: *By Appointment*

Whitewashed coal aches
in the sun along the wharf.
'I name this ship the *Challenger*.

May God preserve her
and all who sail in her . . .'
At the perforated line

of portholes, heavy, clamped,
faces like bottled fruit.
The handpicked crew.

Edward, Prince of Wales,
in uniform at Portsmouth,
is doing his duty.

He lifts one hornet sleeve
and the green skittle
of vintage Bollinger,

a muzzled magnum
with a golden hilt,
smacks against the bows.

Brief cauliflower.
Cheers. Rivets like mangetout.
What a hoot. Cheers.

And now David must dash
to cut a dash tonight
(discreetly, of course)

with Wallis and Ernest
at the Duce's new drama
somewhere in St Martin's Lane.

He can change on his train,
get details from his diary:
Napoleon: The Hundred Days

by Benito Mussolini
and Giovacchino Forzano.
New Theatre (TEM 3878).

He arrives after 9, late,
and enters the perfumed box.
Wallis, ironclad in odour.

He has missed the worst
of Robert Atkins' bombast
from the north cliff of Elba.

Napoleon's second time around
is nearly over. Fouché
instructs Réal in realpolitik:

'Gratitude? In politics,
there is no such thing.'
Soon this Minister of Police

manipulates the deputies
until the elder statesmen,
Jay and Lafayette, demand

the Emperor's abdication.
The critic of *The Times*
already feels for phrases:

'history lies quietly open;
the comment of the Fates;
the audience continuously held'.

In the dark, David finds
and fondles Mrs Simpson's knee.
Vigilant shut-eye for Ernest.

Almost nodding off at 2,
Eliot writes up his diary:
'Two tickets for *Napoleon*,

three shillings each.
Supper at the Trattoria Verde,
five shillings each.

Let me touch her breasts
in the taxi. Nothing more.
No gratitude at all.

Says husband home from sea.
Large investment. No return.
Returned to Maudsley.'

After breast of guinea fowl,
mangetout 'like a battleship',
and quick spinet laughter,

David does embroidery.
'My secret vice,' he says.
Fine surgical stitches,

her eyebrows are attentive,
her crêpe de Chine pleated
like celery. Slender. Hard.

The cotton membrane is pricked,
taut as the cellophane circle
on a jar of preserves.

1932: *Suicide*

The phone is hysterical,
holding its hands
over its ears. Screaming.

Zhenya scratching her face.
Wild cornered eyes
trapped in her head.

Snot in her hair,
on the back of her hand
trying to tear

too many pages at once
of his new book, *Second Birth*,
then roughly smoothing

them out, leaving them
bent. She was suicidal.
He couldn't lift a hand.

Now, from the other room, Zina:
'You answer it. I'm playing
mahjong and she isn't my wife.'

Someone is eating his words.
Can you hear? There.
Soft mastications,

vowels swallowed. Drunk.
'Who is it?' Boris asks,
and hears small, separate

sounds of satisfaction.
A child quenching its thirst.
Sex. Or someone dying. Then,

dazing the metal diaphragm:
'Alleluia, alleluia,
Alliluyeva's shot herself.'

A buzz of ohms. Click.
He lets the telephone fall
and brush the carpet

like the arm of an ape.
He feels sorry for her,
for Stalin, for himself.

He has already thought of this.
Fear has imagined the details,
has made up her mind:

the chip off her tooth
where the sight
was sharp on the barrel,

the rancid taste of oil,
the weighting altered,
tiring her wrists,

hard to hold steady.
She took her own life
while its balance

was disturbed. Thumbs
pressed to the trigger.
So stiff. Then exeunt omnes.

A slogan of blood
daubing the tiles,
ceiling, light bulb, w.c.

It might have been Zhenya.
But when Fadeyev brings
the letter of condolence

for the *Literaturnaya*,
already bearing signatures
of thirty prominent writers,

Boris refuses to sign.
It is too sycophantic.
Soviet Socialist grief.

Zina is beside herself:
'Your name will be missed.
Sign. Everyone signs.'

Boris sips a glass of tea:
'Fadeyev is fond of me.
And I never said why.'

Zina will not come to bed.
She sits playing patience,
keeps a lighted cigarette

between them, her anger
always vigilant. Untouchable.
Unfaltering. Separate. Stone.

'They know what it means.
You say you sympathise.
Then sign. Or go back to her.'

The erotic smack of cards,
insolent slap after slap
in the face, until he writes:

'I share my comrades' feelings.
As a poet, I was there,
seeing and suffering everything.'

His right hand writes
the truth in purple ink.
His left hand is lost

in his hair, philandering,
sending down showers. See.
Drifts, inside and outside.

1933: *Die Viehbremse*

Just a jug in its hairnet.
Alma mater. Plain white china
on the windowsill of 12:13.

Eliot shakes a leg into the leg
of his haunted trousers,
hired only this morning.

Eliot is German learning,
therefore in the accent thinks.
Thinks: that Rilke story,

reciting and rapt.
How did it go again?
He stares at his studs.

'Grossmutters Kleid
hast du getragen,
mit weissen Rosen

und Ärmeln gepufft.
Dein Kleid
aus Grossmutters Tagen.

In den Falten
liegt noch der Duft.'
Something like that.

And the fake falsetto
of Kraus, the Viennese gadfly,
mincing his words:

'Grossvaters Hosen
hast du getragen . . .'
Rilke crushed him with a look.

Eliot crushes his reflection,
his double-ended black bow tie
tweezed and tweaked,

plucked and palped
to a pair of sculls
neat at the neck.

Will Norman remember?
I need your black shoes.
Features slightly unfocused,

a vaseline blurr, listening,
out of breath, to his brother.
Earless. The leather head

solid as a soldier ant,
cased like a cockroach
in his abdominal shield.

A bib of sweat. The gloves
great amber beads on the rope.
An idiot's abacus. The old one-two.

Eliot, in shirtsleeves, paces
the room on staircase 12,
restless as a referee.

The college Visitor crosses
the quad, episcopal gaiters
cracked like a hen's.

Seven strikes. Fellows gather
under the great fig tree.
Fruit cup sways

in its silver bowl
as two college servants
carry it into hall.

Eliot watches from his window.
There's that fruit Jenkins.
Being brilliant, blast him,

with every bone in his body.
Then Eliot has his idea:
black socks over brown shoes,

brave face and bugger Norman.
Later, passing the port,
circumcising a cigar,

Eliot expands and expounds:
'Die Forschungsanstalt
für Psychiatrie at Munich'

(ja, enjoying the German)
'a year doing genetic research.
Rockefeller Foundation funding.

An awfully exciting field.'
He postulates new animals,
biological patents, pedigrees,

bringing back the unicorn,
degeneracy, genetic hygiene,
ideas of the Übermensch.

Clever, modest, considered,
he crosses his legs,
engulfed in an armchair,

and notices, out on a limb,
that one of his shoes
has shed its black sock.

'A little demonstration
of the new genetic science?'
Jenkins asks to general derision.

The pillion passenger
on Norman's belt-driven,
clutchless E. W. Douglas

is a Somerville girl.
Ada Beauchamp, an Eton-cropped
Bollinger Bolshevist.

They've left a ballot box
outside the Oxford Union,
full of white feathers.

Norman wears his jacket
back to front, jokes
about kangaroo petrol,

and begs her to curb
her Marxist leanings
when they take a right turn.

Over a pint she explains.
She can sympathise
with Einstein's four percenters.

She isn't like a college blood.
But there will be a war.
Against the fascists,

not for King and Country.
He is wondering why
his exhaust-valve lifter sticks,

whether she believes
in free love, what her tits
are like, will the condom keep on?

1934: *No Monkey Business*

Seventeen, eighteen, nineteen.
Frau Alias is counting the hairs
in her silverbacked brush,

whose twined initials
cling and copulate,
while Eliot and Yeats

are doing a barn dance,
politely trying to pass
in Eugen Steinach's office door.

Location: Vienna. Above his labs,
fifty-eight, fifty-nine, sixty
Hauptallee, next to the Prater.

It is her daily ritual
because she believes
she is going gradually bald.

Broad black giddyap reins
stream from the poet's pince-nez
during the Gentlemen's Excuse Me:

Entschuldigen Sie, bitte sehr,
diesen Marmeladenverkehr, says Eliot,
before suddenly seeing . . .

Or should I say, he says,
'the struggle of the fly in marmalade'?
Celebrity casts a cold eye

and grandly is gone. At once
replaced by Herr Professor Steinach,
whose Harley Street disciple,

author of *Rejuvenation*, Norman Haire,
has recommended Eliot. And vice versa.
Steinach: perspiring, perfumed,

impatient, emphatic, expository,
vigorous, voluble, Latinate
as Caesar's *Gallic War* Book 7.

(Sixty-one, sixty-two, sixty-three.
Herr Alias is laying down the law,
telling his wife she must come.)

The testicle, Eliot learns,
consists of seminiferous tubules,
whence the semen,

and also polyhedral Leydig cells,
present interstitially,
whence the hormone. Good?

The secret of rejuvenation . . .
(Getting a rise out of W. B. Yeast,
thinks Eliot) the secret of rejuvenation

is proliferation of the hormone.
By one of two quite simple methods.
No monkey business, eh?

(Steinach permits himself
a smile at poor, pitiful Voronoff.)
One: the homoplastic treatment:

grafts on another testicle
in the area of the groin.
The site is scarified,

lightly, with a needle.
The cut surface of the testicle
is laid against the muscle fibres

and the edge of its protective sheath
sewn in place with silk or catgut.
Twelve days' absolute rest.

If it 'takes', more hormone.
Like taking on some extra labour.
First performed by Lespinasse. 1911.

Two: the autoplastic method,
whereby the Leydig cells
are stimulated further

by the tubules having been tied off.
A redirected labour force. Yes?
First performed Uppsala, '94.

(Three, thinks Eliot, bore them rigid.
His features, quelling a yawn,
seem curiously close to a climax.)

Auto-suggestion having to be avoided,
early operations all took place
in the course of other ops,

without the patients
having given their consent.
Friend Lichtenstern, genito-urinary.

The interview is over.
On the stairs, Eliot encounters
a couple, Herr Alias and Frau,

who quarrel in whispers.
He will give her consent
in less than an hour.

And her legs will open to electrodes,
experience their shock,
cold as an earring clasp.

She will give a little scream
and watch the trembling
of the rosewood box,

trapped, as it were,
on the Riesenrad,
between panic and pleasure,

for five or six minutes,
before the professor pronounces
her orgasm achieved.

Choosing his words: this inability,
this incompetence in intercourse,
this clitoral dependency,

amounts to this:
an insult to the penis.
Which will never be forgiven.

1934: *Continuous Performance*

Listening and tilted towards
the clear, quiet evidence
and helter-skelter ringlets

of Irina Alexandrovna Yousoupoff,
Princess of Russia, are:
the Honourable Mr Justice Avory

in shaggy ink cap,
Sir Patrick Hastings K C,
appearing for the plaintiff

in crewcut kite-tailed cauliflower,
and Henry Raine, a juror,
bald as a blackbird's nest.

Hundred percent horsehair wigs,
handwoven, all bobbins and bows,
by Northams, High Street, Oxford;

make-up by Love, Interest and Libel;
sparks by politely cross examination,
conducted 'with all due respect . . .'

Listening and tilted towards
the Prince Yousoupoff,
now resident at Rue Guttenberg,

Boulogne-sur-Seine, Paris,
and (perhaps) Prince Chegodieff
in *Rasputin, The Mad Monk* by MGM:

'How did we murder him?
With cyanide. No, not sodium.
Potassium. Cyanide of potassium.

White crystals pulverised to talc
by Lazovert. Quoi? A doctor. In the army.
Pestle and mortar, grinding its teeth.

I remember his hands. Coldblooded.
Bloodless. From the rubber gloves.
Beige. Like a waxwork.'

Almost his English is perfect.
The accent *is*: eating his words
like caramel toffees, chewing

the diphthongs. Of course.
As a scout, Henry remembers,
in Univ lodge at twilight,

that pas de deux of hands.
That japanned hair like modern art.
Down without a degree. Staircase 9.

Before the war. Opening his vowels,
asking his scout to wind up the goldfish –
an 18 carat hunter kept in water.

'Three almond cakes. Three chocolate.
Under the icing. That is correct.
And in the wines. Madeira. Sauterne,

a Château de Rayne-Vigneau it was,
to mask the cyanide. Of almonds,
my Lord. Bitter, and quite pronounced.

Not Archduke Constantine's Yquem,
but, still, I agree: a perfect waste.
And I don't mean *pourriture noble*, what?

Where was I? Yes. The Starets came.
Grigori Efimovich, down the cellar steps.
With a rustle of cockroaches.

The sound of my own blood.
And I could just make out my voice –
offering the unpoisoned biscuits.

I felt he felt, when our eyes met,
the scald of knowledge in my own.
And all he did was smile.

Have a seat, I said. I will, he said.
The wickerwork mewed like a kitten.
Silence, then upstairs

the others, the others started
with the gramophone. "Yankee Doodle".
Again and again. Hysterical.

Like someone washing their hands.
Or laughing. Or sobbing. Inconsolable.
Compulsive. The ancient mariner.

He held me with his glittering eye,
drank off the poisoned glass
and ate two cakes. And lived:

he drooped; he did not die;
he wanted me to play guitar.
As well as "Yankee Doodle". Aie.

Someone failing to find the spot,
that's what I was like.
Left a bit. Down a bit. No.

Itching the chords, seeking,
scratching for Scarlatti,
fretting the frets.

Left a bit. Down a bit. Yes:
I could see his chin, yes,
descend like a violinist.

Then came the slow movements
of his breath. It was half past two.
I went upstairs to get a gun.

Cards on the green card-table,
as if they were sitting an exam.
They seemed not like ones who'd failed,

but like ones who had succeeded
only in arranging for an aegrotat.'
The allusion lost on everyone,

including Henry, who is out of sorts,
as if (acid asides inside)
he's eaten something disputatious.

'When the others heard the shot,
someone, in the rush to help,
brushed up against the switch.

Strange. Darkness wasn't dark.
I couldn't see, but I was seeing red.'
Henry nods; agrees; comes back.

'An eyelid moved. His left.
Then nothing moved. I couldn't tell.
It wasn't like a lizard,

when we distinguish states
of stillness and arrest. You know?
I bent down to take a closer look

and felt his fist tighten.
I screamed and left my epaulette
behind. Uprooted. Broken threads.

Like a gardener clutching a clod,
weeding a flowerbed,
the Starets knelt a moment.

No, I admit that I was terrified.
The wound? Yes, it was visible.
He wore a white silk blouse.

Less than you might think.
I'd say more like the mark
left by the new ball

on a pair of flannels.
Well, we locked him in
and he broke down the door.

Finally? Purishkevich shot him.
Out in the snow. Several times.
A press? A loaded stick.

I used one on the Starets' head.
Unrecognisable? No. Disreputable.
As if he'd been in a drunken brawl.

Bundled in a blue velvet curtain.
Dropped into the Neva from a bridge.
Which one? I couldn't say.

I wasn't there. I stayed behind.
To remove all traces of the murder.
Camphor on the bloodstains.

Outside, oil-paint tinted like the flags.
Blood analysis? Of course.
A single shot behind the ear for Scout.

The name I gave the chow we had.
A beauty. Black tongue. Springy cinnamon
like yarn. A party-squeaker tail.

Coiled. What we Russians call
stepmothers' tongues. A pedigree:
Hsuan Tsung, Emperor of Tweeddale.

We called him Scout.'
Henry, unlike the Prince, is untouched
by this veterinarian tenderness.

Feeling ebbs from his finger-ends.
They look as dead as candle-grease,
the colour of a marble font.

Call Mrs Elise Mary Budd of Brighton,
film-goer and unprofessional Russophile,
who will testify she thought:

Chegodieff was Yousoupoff.
And that, therefore, therefore,
therefore Princess Chegodieff

(seduced by Grishka Rasputin
before she marries Chegodieff
in the final thrilling reel)

was in real life the Princess Yousoupoff.
Which is a costly libel,
priced at five and twenty thousand pound,

owing to the plaintiff's social eminence,
as argued by Sir Patrick Hastings:
'If a Mr Smith of Balham

is arrested by mistake tonight,
the news might rate a minor notice
and his damages be small.

But if Sir William Jowitt . . .'
Laughter in court.
Jowitt is the silk for M G M.

Henry, feeling poorly, reflects:
beauty and good luggage
always carry the day.

Ironical. The mockery.
This successful libel suit
was instigated by a murderer.

Laughter in court.
But not in the Imperial Court.
Grigori Efimovich Rasputin:

pedigree: saviour of the Caesarevitch,
friend of Badmaev the Tibetan lama,
mesmerist, faith healer, Khlyst.

Henry contemplates his headgear,
lined with silk like a coffin,
where the soul survives:

the tiniest
black barathea butterfly
balanced on the leather headband.

1934: *Standard Bread*

A ceremonial progress,
acclaimed and heckled,
through the body of the hall,

like a steady icebreaker
creating this splinter of arms,
salutes that swell and subside.

From up on the ceiling
(where else?) Olympia presents
Sir Oswald Mosley,

a home perm of seats,
and the pong of hydrogen sulphide
from the Communist stink bombs.

Sir Oswald is a damn good egg.
Or else. A blackshirt bouncer
adjusts and tightens a touch

the knot of Jimmy's red tie,
draws on his fag (*ecco*,
as a chef acclaims a dish

by kissing off his fingertips)
then fumigates
the tie's contaminated colour.

Suspect, from his aisle seat,
Jimmy affects an interest
in the woman sitting next to him.

The wealth of her flanks
redistributed, with the sound
of intaken breath,

Jimmy observes the nub
of her left front suspender,
swells, salutes, thank God subsides.

The houselights, too, are lowered.
Poised to speak at the lectern,
in a test-tube of light,

Mosley lingers for silence
in silence, only to hear
the barracking begin.

A blinkered spot sweeps,
blazes like a compass card
of splintered light,

and settles the trouble
there at South East by South
by bringing the blackshirts

like a swarm of flies to shit.
North North West. East by South.
East by North. South West by West.

An hour's delay for ejections
like sandhoppers into Hammersmith Road.
Then the trouble dies down.

'We are grateful,' Mosley begins,
'to those few people
who have been interrupting.

They show the pressing need
to protect free speech
by a proper Fascist Defence Force.'

The woman at Jimmy's elbow
starts to scream and thrash.
It is an epileptic fit,

but the steward smacks her face,
forehand, backhand, forehand,
till her nose begins to bleed.

Helps her out by the tits.
Throwing her handbag after.
It is sick on the pavement.

A Barclays chequebook. Scent.
A charm bracelet. Lipstick.
An opened envelope.

Then the exit closes
as the blackshirt brings
its iron bar banging down.

And afterwards, some comrades
infiltrate the lectern area
and sway the podium itself.

Later still, a cheeky figure
in the girders of the roof
whistles the Internationale

and brings Sir Oswald to a stop.
Ankles crossed, he asks,
before he disappears:

'Are you the same Mosley
who thought up Standard Bread?'
A climbing steward comes unstuck.

Jimmy sees all this
and doesn't see all this,
since what he sees

is what he watched
as if it were a tennis match.
Forehand, backhand, forehand.

In Bombay, in Calcutta,
in Rangoon, in Penang, in Batavia.
All points of the compass: Jim.

1934: *Answer the Telephone*

Stella and Stella's new breasts
are taking their weekly bath,
monitored by Stella's family.

The full, adoring complement:
perspiring Papa, proud Mama,
little sister, little brother,

and big brother are watching
the delicate, blunt beauty
of her breasts, nipples

like dregs of rosé,
deliciously inaccessible.
Each aureole pricked out.

When the communal telephone rings
in the hall's camera obscura.
For Boris Leonidovich.

Who is fetched and finds himself
staring at Stella's wet breasts
through a pinhole in the plaster

and talking to Comrade Stalin.
Swung gleam. (What?) Each tit
tipped like a billiard cue

with pink morocco plush.
They hold their audience.
What? He stares up the wall,

away from the hairy hole,
at Papa's portrait of Tolstoy,
old L. N. in his linen *rubashka*

like a German dentist,
hung high in the darkness.
And what does Borya feel?

Power. Most of all, power.
Peter the Great, pulling out
teeth, teeth by the sackful.

His own begin to ache,
steadily, like testicles
after hours of foreplay.

And in himself? Power, too,
importance, panic. Pride and fear.
Excitement almost sexual.

He has the sense
that everything is clear,
intimate, but upside down.

When Stalin mentions Mandelstam,
Boris feels, profoundly feels
there must be some mistake.

Is Mandelstam a genius?
(Osip Emilyevich? *Mandelstam?*
But what about me?)

Disappointed, downcast, genuine,
Boris addresses the question:
a good writer, yes. A *genius* . . .

His voice trails off.
Trails off, he suddenly thinks,
like drops of blood

and sees them there,
splintered on the parquet floor,
as he sees the question,

at last, for what it is.
Political. And therefore:
Osip Emilyevich is a poet

and a poet who will live
as long as Russian poetry.
Against the sentence of death,

pronounces this short sentence.
He will forget the exact words
because (for him) they are untrue.

He will remember only the truth.
The things he thought.
The sense of being chosen.

The shameful sense of eagerness,
of having said too much.
Of unrequited love.

Hello? Hello? Hello? Hello?
Outside, the full moon hangs up
her radical mastectomy.

Epileptic by the geyser,
a fly, unable, injured
on its trampoline. Poised,

the doctor's black bag
hesitates, then hurries to help,
with eight horrible handles.

1935: *Draw that Fuse*

Henry, hunched in the park,
unable to lift his head, seeing
only the broad swung scythe

of a woman's tweed skirts
and the red brick base
of the bandstand's cast-iron crown.

The weight of his head
deep sunk on his chest,
though his eyes are alert

to the tiny stars
crushed in the asphalt.
Lips slurred in saliva

like someone asleep.
Like Alderman Horace Dainty,
'elder and lifelong member'

of the Wesley Memorial Church,
'who sleeps at peace
in the arms of the Father',

commemorated by this iron stereotype
above the lead-tagged fuse box,
where Jimmy tries to learn

his boss's son about electric:
'electric can't be heard,
it can't be seen, it can't be smelt.

You don't know if it's there.
So if you play with it,
for badness or a joke,

watch out: there's something
sharp and prickly in the wires,
that jumps out up your arm.'

Little Billy, four years old,
plugs in his thumb. Learned.
His father, Tallentyre,

reaches in his hessian tool sling
spread like a lake, and rummages,
then extends his fists:

'Right on, then, choose.
We can't get on till electric's off.
I've give Matt Newby

price of two pints
to look the other way. Pick.'
And Jimmy picks the paper twist

of half-inch nails, so loses.
Even with the Electric's foreman
squared, he is reluctant.

'Draw that fuse,' says Tallentyre,
'or get your cards.'
Jimmy draws the fuse.

A sword sheathed in his arm,
the alternating current
throws him right across the church,

backwards, like film
ripped out of a projector.
Laughing, Tallentyre wipes his eyes:

'The Keystone Kops. Hell,
you should've seen yourself.
Who's that nigger? Jesse Owens.'

John Cleveland Owens, actually,
Ohio State, I fuss for the record,
long jump, broad jump, take your pick.

The stop-cock fixed, flood contained,
it's Tallentyre's turn,
since Jimmy has refused the fuse.

'Give it *here*.' Before his son, bravado.
He presses home the point
and is hard-pressed. Held. Fused.

Flypaper. His teeth buzz.
His body curves, shaking, urgent
as a mongrel fucking in the street.

His baby teeth a bracelet,
an ivory oval in the gloom,
little Billy starts to laugh,

helpless, in the grip, oblivious
to the smell of cooking meat:
his father's fingers. Tallentyre,

dragged by Jimmy by his jacket
off the mains, still holds the fuse.
'What a bastard.' He wags his hand.

'Get the bastard back with sticks.'
And so they do. He does.
Without a word of thanks.

Like a man about to squeeze
into the needle's squint,
Henry Raine is shrinking,

away from something invisible,
inaudible, a prickle in his blood,
bad smells he now hallucinates.

1935: *Hot Air Mail*

Mutualité, Palais de la, Paris.
Admiration, mutual in.
Russian, idioms for emphasis

in argument, include:
needless to say, to say the least,
and by the way, and in the first place.

Tsvetaeva, Marina Ivanovna,
sexuality of, strong with Sapphic
variations (*see* Parnok, Sophia),

encounters Pasternak, B. L.,
transfiguration of, *see* suit,
arranged by Stalin's secretary

erroneously, egregiously
(*vide infra* inside leg, *supra* sleeves)
amusingly (*see* teeth, tobacco stained).

For the past, *see* Correspondence,
acrostic in *Lieutenant Schmidt*,
altered archive dedication

to Pasternak of *After Russia*:
'my brother in the fifth season,
sixth sense and fourth dimension'.

As for the present tense,
it relaxes in the corridors
of powerlessness, the index

of this international conference
defending culture from the fascists,
and it collapses into laughter

at his 'epileptic' suit,
the stumble in her hem,
burns left by her cigarettes,

confirming Yablonovsky's verdict
on her verse: 'she enters literature
in curlers and a dressing gown.'

More breathless, gasping laughter,
her hand on his arm, begging,
soul mates in the flesh,

until he takes her by the nose
between the knuckles of his hand,
laughing, leads her to his lips.

Corrida in the corridors,
their two bodies flirt,
dancing with the danger of each other.

Observed, complacently, by Efron,
contented cuckold, and Mr B,
eyes and ears of the NKVD,

who are one and the same,
both placid in the knowledge
that, now his hands are full,

Pasternak's preoccupation
with Marinochka and poetry
will reduce the risk of intercourse

with Whites, to say the least.
The whereabouts of Pasternak?
Out of breath. Under her bum.

Or is about to be, thinks Efron,
the snug fit of his (face)
like a flute in its case.

By train from Quai d'Orsay
to Meudon, Clamart by bus,
so Tsvetaeva can pack

her gosling weekend case
for Saint-Gilles-sur-Vie.
Sweeping armfuls like a burglar:

her diaphragm, two flyswats
'useful for beach badminton',
a shuttlecock like Sitting Bull,

her bathing dress and Efron's suit.
Thus Borya running backwards to the sea,
lest she should spot his spotty back.

And the chalet later,
sand-strewn, cold, self-catering,
cognac, conversation, kissing,

then Borya unbuttoned, laughing,
naked, twilit, laughing, lithe,
doing Vaslav Nijinsky in *L'Après-midi*...

She will never forget
the squeak of his dancing feet,
ghosts in the ignorant lino.

She will never forget
the one grey hair
she found or what she said:

Borya, when you are old,
with an old man's smouldering ears,
there will be fire in your heart.

She will never forget
how afterwards she spoke:
what will we do?

And his unforgettable reply:
we will forget this happened.
Censored. Needless to say.

On his return, out of his senses,
he doesn't tell his wife he's back,
proposes to Akhmatova in Leningrad.

1935: *Who was Bismarck?*

München: the Danish consul
confers a single, swaddled rose
on every female guest.

Outside, it is November,
minus drei, newspapers
gathered by an officious wind.

Frost deep-fries the ferns
in the Hofgarten walks. White
rust. Neglected in their window box,

six suedette chrysanthemums
reproach the consular hothouse
like a model aeroplane:

balsa struts, taut tissue
transparent with dope, unpainted,
grounded, ready for take-off.

Seeing the thornless rose
in his fiancée's hand, Eliot,
brooding on breeding, thinks:

thorny subject, racial hygiene.
(And, observing the innocent cut
of the consular eggcup trousers:

Nothing *there* to sterilise.)
Why, after the United States,
does *Denmark* lead the field?

Why does Germany come third?
Why? Because. Several reasons.
Resistance since the law was passed:

appeals clog up the machinery.
That Bavarian Catholic pamphlet:
appeal in *every* case. What else?

Doctors dislike notification:
relatives of reported patients
take their custom to another practice.

Defectives, dipsos, epileptics,
psychos, schizos, deviants, etc.
all risk being sterilised

should the defect be deemed congenital:
women at a thousand marks,
men between one and two hundred marks.

(Prognathous. Pouting. Petulant.
Pin-eyed. Pop-eyed. Pathological.
Tropical fish fan themselves.)

Subject to due legal process
before the court (*Erbgesundheitsgericht*),
the case is certified

O K (*erblich belastet*) or not,
depending on the evidence
(*der Antrag*) assembled

by the district officer for health.
E.g. answers to 'elementary' questions:
When is Christmas? Who was Bismarck?

What is the simple interest
on the sum of 300 marks
at 3% for seven years?

What is truth? Make a sentence
using these three words:
'soldier', 'war', 'fatherland'.

Then, this last October,
marriage laws and marriage loans.
Dwarfs (less than 130 cm.)

not eligible for loans
or tax relief for children.
Jews disqualified as well.

And restricted to specific partners:
full Jews must marry full Jews only;
half Jews must marry full Jews only.

Practising half Jews count as full Jews.
Quarter Jews must marry Aryans.
This consulate is full of Jews.

Including Eliot's fiancée,
Lydia Leonidovna Pasternak,
who is dancing to the wireless,

who represents not passion
but scientific principle.
Her 'tainted' Jewish blood

is excellent genetic stock.
Besides (he ticks them off),
as daughter of a famous artist

and a former concert pianist,
as sister of a leading poet,
bourgeois breeding with bohemia,

she speaks to Eliot's snobbery.
Social snobbery, not sexual.
His appetites are delicate.

Leonid has painted his portrait.
Eyes asleep, brushwork mimed
like the ticking tail

of a cat caught by its prey.
And also the sparrow's r.e.m.
from sitter to easel to sitter.

Refusing Eliot's (agreed) 300 marks
as utterly inadequate:
'Please regard it as a gift.'

Or as an obligation.
Look at Lydia now. Laughing.
Strong, sun-tanned features,

somehow slightly masculine.
Her double chin, her heavy nose.
Is Eliot anti-Semitic, too?

Laughing like a horse.
Flat, unspankable buttocks.
Large aureoles on tiny breasts.

Unlike his gold engagement ring,
she isn't made to measure.
Eliot imagines the ring

next to the red carbolic soap
in the w.c. of the Berlin express,
where he left it – by chance.

Why is her body so square?
The innocent cut of his jib,
his lifeless twelve-inch fly

flat as a mangetout.
His 'gold' Kensitas coupons watch
reminds him of mortality.

Once more unto the breach.
Youth's a thing will not endure.
He is marrying for children.

And in a week, a week,
to England with his bride-to-be,
leaving behind the Institute,

and all the Hitler photographs
hung by brownshirt 'scientists'
instead of 'Jewish daubs' by Pasternak,

his lab mice whistling like a kettle,
murmuring to Lang in a moving lift,
sitting, in silence, Russian-style,

before the journey begins,
with Karlchen on his knee,
with Lenchen astride Lydia,

and everyone crying in silence,
except for Eliot,
Eliot icy with altruism

(that notice at Seeshaupt:
Juden nicht erwünscht)
mired in his own mistake.

1936: *Du bist wie eine Jude*

A six-place white bone china setting,
set for Fedya, Zhonya, Karlchen, Lenchen.
No guests. And no female servants

since the law today forbidding
Aryan girls all jobs in Jewish households.
Lest paterfamilias gets familiar.

And Karlchen is inconsolable:
Ilse whom he loves has left,
without a reason. Just goodbye.

Because Karlchen and Lenchen
have no idea they are Jews,
that their father, Frederick,

vice-president of the Vereinsbank,
is etc., etc. Their mother, too.
Only Fedya looks as if etc., etc.

The plates of lentil soup,
identical, a daisy chain
of *Koenigszell* silesian china,

getting cold as Karlchen cries
thick, acid tears, his hot face
constipated with emotion.

She is sixteen, he is six.
Hugging her knees in bed,
the patient exposition of her past,

its endless intricate etc., etc.
and when she lets her earphones down,
she lets him feel her flaxen flex,

and what he feels is love,
'when even if the journey's long
it only takes a minute'.

The thought of her teeth,
crooked, white, wet,
the unbroken bow of her eyebrows,

and he is shaken with silent sobs
like the hiccoughs of boats
at their moorings.

It is snowing outside:
rivel-ravel cross-eyed ticker-tape.
The curtains are open.

Then stillness and the soufflé
on the saddle of a bike.
Karlchen crying like a taxi.

To cheer him up, the butler, Heinrich,
impersonates a one-man band.
Never known to fail.

Each hand shakes a silver tablespoon
stuck in a bottle, while he bangs
the door behind him with his heel,

spraying spittle from his lips
which fart the 'tune'. A 'tune'.
Definitely the indefinite article.

And when this distraction doesn't work?
Lenchen loses patience with her brother:
Du bist wie eine Jude! Scathingly.

Fedya. Zhonya. Karlchen. Heinrich.
Silence and the snow's drop-shadow lettering.
Lenchen. The buzz of conversation stopped.

1936: *Matty, the Acem Giant*

On the washroom cistern,
a dried sliver of carbolic soap,
crisp as a dental plate.

Cautious, duck-lipped,
Matty's mouth approaches
his coffee. And stops.

A tightpuckeredtarpaulinofskin.
His fissured finger fishes out
the offence like a used French letter.

Lays it next to the soap.
The washbasin, ermine
with oily fingerprints.

At least he is able to drink
without using a straw.
Matty surveys his damaged face,

freckled in the dusty mirror,
marked and chipped
as the mirror is marked.

How are the mighty fallen,
in the midst of sparring
with that little cunt Raine.

Slain in thine high places.
Like splinters under the skin,
spelks, his healing cuts.

Stitches like false eyelashes
under his eyelashes. Left eye
still closed like buttocks,

cleavage the colour of beer.
Shards sharp to his short tongue.
No sword in his hand,

the little cunt Raine,
just bare fists at lunch break.
It was Matty's own idea:

'Tell me yerra bit of a boxther.
What about a bit of thparrin'?
Put a thyow on for the ladth.'

'You're too big for me, Matty.'
(True. Bigger by more than a foot.
Question: how did Raine manage

to mark Matty's face? So much.
Answer: he didn't dare miss.)
'Whath the matter? Are yer yeller?'

And Norman's jacket was off,
jerked to the workshop corner,
one sleeve half inside out:

'Matty, if I was only five stone,
I wouldn't be frightened of you.'
The men in the paint shop made a ring,

and in less than ten minutes
Raine made a monkey out of his face.
Now Matty sips at his mug,

turns into the paint shop again,
where Norman is waiting,
a huge wisp of hubris:

'Fancy another bit sparring?'
It's an offer Matty cannot refuse
without losing face, but then,

he hasn't much face left to lose.
Putting his coffee carefully down,
for answer, he picks up one-handed

an internal-expanding buffer
and swings its hundredweight of steel
onto a shelf above his head:

'What about a wrethling match inthtead?'
Norman sees the magic carpet of dirt,
the trickle of rust from the shelf,

and nods a silent nod, thinking,
'Serves you right, you silly sod'
and 'What the fuck did you say that for?'

The Acem Giant folds him in a hug,
sweeps him off his feet.
Has a crush on him.

Ribs. Impossible to breathe.
Dangling legs. Ventriloquist
and ventriloquist's dummy.

So, before he blacks out,
with clenched fists,
Norman clashes both his temples.

How the mighty are fallen. Again.
Percussion. Brain between buffers.
Matty is prone on the dribbled floor,

arms outstretched, his biceps
veined, engorged, as breasts
are muscular with milk.

Norman is wearing his work boots
with cast-iron heel cleats.
Teeth clenched, a long jumper,

he jumps both heels at once
into the biceps,
grunting with effort.

Bloodless, blueblack cusps appear,
willow-pattern, oiled with whey.
Norman looks at the useless arms,

hears the noise of his heart
like the clump of a flagstone.
Sits, a mahout on Matty's chest,

the heels of his hands
pushing the giant's chin.
'Give in, Matty.'

Matty shakes his head.
'Give in. I'll break your neck.'
Coarse with pores, the tautened skin,

veins visible like a lizard
under the scarlet skin,
a tent of tendons.

'I'll break your bloody neck.'
The works' buzzer goes for work,
then stops.

But Norman presses on,
until the Acem Giant gasps,
'Give in, ah give in.'

Norman leads him,
like Lazarus back from the dead,
to Mr Wells Hood, the manager.

Knocks on the glass door.
'Enter.' Wells Hood at ease
in front of his stilton fireplace.

Norman beckons Matty forward.
'I want to know who set him on.
And I want a witness, sir.

Who set you on to me?'
Silence. The Acem Giant's tongue,
a swab on swollen lips.

'Matty, lift your arms.'
'Ah can't.' 'How will you stop me
hitting your face, Matty?'

Pinstripe suit and pinstripe hair,
the horrified Wells Hood protests,
'For God's sake, Raine, please no.'

Is overridden by Raine,
whose fist is drawn back:
'I'll count to ten.'

The cause is lost in history,
a feud between two men long dead;
their living genealogy of blame

culminates with Norman's curse:
'I hope your arsehole moves
into the middle of your body,

so that every time you shit
you have to get undressed.'
It will. In six months' time.

For once, I see ahead.
I see the exit wound erupt.
Gouged, milled, ground, minced.

Some nobody will pull the trigger,
bullied beyond endurance.
Below the left nipple, a sphincter.

1936: *A Bit of Abyssinia in Bath*

While Jimmy brushes up
the Word of God
(the letter, not the spirit),

Haile Selassie the First,
formerly Ras Tafari Makonnen,
grand-nephew of Menelik the Second,

111th descendant of Solomon
and of Sheba, now Negus,
yea, Negusa Nagast,

Elect of God, yea,
conquering Lion of Judah,
and also, to the locals,

a 'little coloured man',
immaculate in bowler hat,
dark suit and cape,

sovereign of several sticks,
for church, for town,
for inspecting non-existent troops,

absolute Abyssinian monarch,
subject to severe attacks
of irritable bowel,

is taking a windy, wintry walk
from Fairfield to Bath,
his constitutional,

with Colonel Roniger
three steps behind,
past, first, the cemetery,

past Comfortable Buildings,
past Albion Terrace, past
the Bath Gas-Light & Coke Co.

(owed money by the Emperor)
then past the rusty trio
of turquoise gasometers

(not unlike, thinks Roniger,
the hatboxes from Harrods
flung out of the palace,

with stiff-starched collars
and yards of Liberty prints,
by the rank rank-and-file

of the defeated Ethiopian army,
deserted by its Emperor,
who had taken a train

at Akaki, ten miles from Addis,
crossed the river to Dire Dawa,
and halted in the heat

for several hours in the heat
before crossing the Danakil Desert,
diddley-dum, diddley-dee, into exile,

taking the rheumatic Empress,
her pet papillon puppy,
the silent Crown Prince,

the tearful Duke of Harar,
Prince Sahle Selassie,
the Princess Tananye,

and the Princess Tsahai
to work as a probationer
Great Ormond Street nurse)

until they reach, as usual,
the Ebenezer Chapel,
built in 1910, whose pyramid roof

is covered with quotations
taken from the Holy Bible,
one of which,

YE

MUST   BE

BORN   AGAIN

Jimmy Raine is repainting white,
the one whose sentiment
the Emperor takes to heart

and stares at hours on end,
while Roniger remembers
how the war was lost:

Selassie's Aero-hair
a swarm of flies, heat,
his rows of medal ribbons

like a paintbox, heat,
paying scavengers (with silk shirts,
dollars, satin capes) to skirmish

while the feasting chiefs
drank tej and ate from massobs,
and were demoralised by rain

and by marauding Azebu Galla,
until the Emperor broke off
the war for pilgrimage

to all eleven churches of Lalibala,
each one carved in solid rock,
eating only injera and water,

and afterwards on to Addis
where the war drum of Menelik
was beaten brutally two whole hours

before the Emperor took the train
which took him to the *Enterprise*,
a British cruiser off Jibuti:

all of which Roniger remembers,
watching the Emperor's gaze
glittering like the broken glass

spread by Badoglio's troops,
a kilometre cordon
against the Abyssinian foot,

watching the splosh of white
jump like jism from Jimmy's brush,
waved like a flywhisk at the Emperor,

his complicated pride unbroken
by the bump and grind
of bolts of Liberty prints,

collars scattered like fingernails,
Baldwin's broken promises,
or unpaid gas and electric bills.

1936: *Hold Your Hand Out, You Naughty Boy*

Windowless, high-ceilinged,
the cold, distempered dressing room
has seen it all. The one chair,

Co-op cane, over-pliant.
The cold radiator. The basin,
clean, because there is no plug.

The one metal locker,
chipped beige paint, scarred
tribally with ventilation slats.

A scroll of canvas stretcher.
Thin-skinned boxing boots
fainted full-length, taking a dive.

And mummified fists,
pot, hard as a lavatory pan
when sweat sets

the plaster of Paris, dusted
into three-inch cotton bandages
before the bout. Like seasoning.

Two hard cases
in two 8 oz. gloves.
Punching more than your weight.

And undetectable, unless
the referee not only feels
but also smacks the bandages –

quite hard. And not always then.
The boxers keep them clenched.
One cough of dust disqualifies.

Later, in the dressing room,
the 'spats' are sawn off
with a hacksaw blade

the colours of iodine,
its frayed edge
an edge of bandage, petrified.

The evidence becomes
a bit of builder's rubble
in a Boots Cash Chemist bag

dropped from the train back home.
Seeing the saw, Norman decides:
give up the game professionally,

get reinstated amateur. Because.
Because he is disgusted. Morally.
Because he was beaten last week

for a shot at the title:
the taste of gumshield
like a rubber johnny in his mouth.

Because this dressing room.
Because prizes are better than purses.
Cases of cutlery. Sherry glasses.

A six-place china dinner service.
Because this dressing room.
Outside, the evening star

shining like a money spider.
To train by the sea again:
that greyhound's dashed-off signature,

one corner of a cornfield
franked with poppies,
that hare crouched like a moth,

sudden bouts of conducting,
and a tree creeper, there,
tight to the trunk,

see its quick spiral
like a roll of bandage
melting in the second's hand.

1937: *Black Sheep*

Late May in the Moscow boulevards:
the chestnut in its convict clothes
and Mandelstam like Lazarus,

returned from Voronezh,
and constantly getting the giggles,
bucked by being back (back!)

after three years in exile.
The process of arrest arrested,
Article 58 behind him at last.

Back! His flat has been faithful:
bare floorboards luxurious,
grained like smoked salmon

under their half-inch permafrost.
He wipes a fan of floor clean
with his overcoat sleeve,

frayed cuff freshly trimmed.
Spiders sprawl in their hammocks.
The radiator hot. Hot for three years!

But his body has gone bad:
along the ripe eyelids
amber granules of glue,

boils on the back of his neck,
peeled, shining, unplugged,
and the lips composing, composing.

To Borya, gone field-grey himself,
giggling: the menu's changed,
we're in a vegetarian phase.

Once I saw a flock of sheep
being forced into the abattoir.
Their sides were heaving,

but the faces gave nothing away.
I wondered what they looked like
underneath their masks.

Mandelstam, a filthy fledgling,
transparent, lips composing
even as he stops, afraid,

hearing the lift. Giggling.
Fear makes you impotent.
We've said enough to get ten years.

For our wives to stand in a prison queue,
next to the names beginning with M
and all the others starting with P.

Arsehole puce under the eyes.
Clammy calyx of hair
clagged to his wet skull.

Like the lip of a jug
this bulging Bourbon bottom lip,
composing, decomposing.

1937: *A Room for Roniger*

Well-oiled. Roniger and Jimm. Y.
Like a lump of butter
drunk in the frying pan.

Legless. Slowly. Dying. Henry.
Sunk in his shawl, in himself,
in front of the fire.

Like a man staring out
at the flight of a bumble-bee,
a shrinking semibreve

lost in the loops and threads
of shorthand filling his sight.
Facing the music. Knowing the score.

He cannot be distracted now.
He wants to know the answer:
O death where is thy sting?

He could take precautions.
If he knew. His words slurred.
Buzzers a scissors.

In the kitchen, Queenie listens,
as Jimmy. Explains. That Roniger.
Just as much a refugee as Lydia.

Who is upstairs, washing her hair
and crying. Soap gets in your eyes.
Choked with limescale,

the shower set speaks
its spider of spray. Cautious.
Long distance. Spindly. Faint.

Eliot hasn't touched her
since their honeymoon.
And then only once in a week.

An icy week at Ilfracombe.
Half way through he fell alseep.
Or pretended to. Suddenly soft.

Sunrise at 6 by her wristwatch.
Watching the wallpaper,
finding Jewish profiles hidden there,

she heard him masturbating
in the other bed. A whisper
on the linen sheets like breath,

like Henry's breathing now,
careful, almost surreptitious,
trying to suppress the shudder.

What's the difference? In the end?
Italian fascism. German. Therefore.
Therefore *en-titled* to a room.

Peas keep falling off his forks,
so Jimmy lowers his face. Too close.
The whole weight of his head

crashes into the brisket of beef,
the mash, the peas, the sprouts.
Grounded in gravy, he sleeps.

The law of inertia, says Roniger,
is difficult to judge.
Your son, says Roniger, I understand,

has invented the drop-shadow lettering?
Such solemn conversation,
he and Queenie burst out laughing.

Upstairs, Eliot blots his diary:
Father's colon doesn't differentiate
solid waste from gas. Crying

about the butterfly of excrement
blotted into his pyjama bottoms.
Difficulties feeding now.

Swallow reflex non-existent.
I wish that I could say to him
how much I love him. Before he dies.

The room for Roniger
will be arranged tomorrow.
He and Jimmy share a bed tonight.

Therefore. They turn and touch.
As thick as thieves. Solid spam.
Jimmy makes a meal of it. Garlic.

Catching the come in his hand,
the consistency of starch.
Wanking off with it.

1937: *A Prison Visit*

In der kleiner Führer,
das Strafgefängnis Plötzensee
where poor Kroll has been detained

is at D 2. The end of the tramline.
And then a walk through a wood
with a woodpecker snoring.

Along an edge of canal:
oil like tarnished silver,
burnt Tyrian iodines,

towpath coaldust underfoot,
jet hundreds-and-thousands
like beading on an evening bag.

Leonid contemplates the door,
studded, like a ham with cloves,
and the door within the door.

His gloved finger
on the mint imperial
at first summons silence –

the woodpecker snoring –
then a hawking of keys
and the shutter spat back.

Leonid's visiting permit
is plucked from his hand.
The shutter sniffs shut.

The guardroom's great library.
Row on row on row on row of keys,
hung from iron hoops:

sprats, frozen waterfalls,
fighting fans, false Triton beards,
axes, adzes, halberds, hatchets.

A coil of quarter-inch rope
as a lighter for cigarettes:
its smouldering chancre.

And then poor Kroll,
tearful, still testing the hair
over his bald patch,

one eye like a Victoria plum.
Unshaven weak brown bristles
like a kiwi fruit.

Beltless, tieless, laceless.
His Latvian passport confiscated.
His consultancy with KDW kaput.

Convicted of convictions:
part of a solicitors' ring
for getting Judengeld out of Germany.

And now his son:
tell Sasha to leave for London.
Natasha teaches at the Reimann School.

(So the son will be safe
with his sister, Leonid thinks,
but what about the wife?) And Zolya?

Unpersuadable. She stays.
We're letting Bayreuthstrasse.
She'll help out at Dambachtal.

Three years. It could be worse.
Leonid points to his own eye
and at the question there.

Nothing serious. Another prisoner.
When I wouldn't . . . A pervert type.
I know I look like death.

No, Leonid thinks. Not death.
But cobwebbed with cracks.
And close enough. To tears.

For long. For. Pauses. Reflection.
Lights gather in the eyes.
Panes brighten and break.

And yet until the time is up,
they carry on a conversation:
Kroll's cell contains a Felix Krull

whose cover is a Catholic priest.
Years ago, he used to do a rabbi.
It died the death with Hitler.

A silk bookmark of hair
flat between Kroll's breasts,
fine as threads on a cob of maize.

1937: *Arrested for Murder*

Hearing the hinge of the peacock,
Norman, arrested, amazed by the maze.
Of moss, two millimetres high.

The green blueprint of a maze,
and there, at the centre, a bee,
groping stone, like the Minotaur.

He hadn't realised the maze was there.
While Olive was shelling canoes,
long ships for lunch, he looked around.

Now Mrs Pretty walks towards him
like a buckled wheel. Polio.
The click and creak of her caliper.

Like a bee in her fox fur wrap,
her polished bun
quilted under its hairnet.

'I can see you've found it.
You're Olive's friend from Oxford.
It's a different make of maze:

always getting lost itself.
We have to weed like anything,
or else it disappears. Poof.

All the gardeners think it tiresome,
I think. Especially Spooner.
But it brings my father back.'

Spooner? The Romeo she complained about.
Playing pocket billiards.
Pointed comments when she rubbed

the Jacobean candlesticks.
'Your father?' Norman asks.
'Designed the thing before he died.

It's supposed to be a rose.
That's why the bee. Did you work it out?'
And Norman: 'No. I see it now.'

Exhausted what they have to say.
The house in its ivy pullover.
Rusty bedsprings of bracken.

Silence. So he volunteers:
'Those cyst things on the heath
should be investigated.'

But then the constable arrives
by bicycle from Woodbridge
and takes the winded Norman

into custody: a charge of murder.
A hand on his shoulder,
he turns like someone waking

from the workings of a poem.
Suddenly sees a whole lost world:
that slow worm's stylus,

one eye's pin-prick of blood,
and its slow bronze bending,
the ferry's cloak of ripples,

the constable's helmet,
its freeze-dried dust
of rough blue serge,

the badge a monstrance,
and the helmet's dim interior:
cathedral light of wintergreen,

two bright bodkins stabbing
through the ventilation holes,
on cracked green linen glaze

the owner's name inscribed
and worn away with sweat to Greek.
Eyelets left by feeding fish.

The ink pad fills its tin
exactly. Curved at the corners.
Spongy to touch. Cake mix gone corrupt.

Press down. Transfer. Press down.
And roll. Left side. Right side.
Black frost-bitten finger-ends.

Then Eliot on the telephone
confirms his brother's alibi.
The unnipped nip of handcuffs.

A mug of good strong tea,
of tea with poke in it
to perk you up. Boxers' tea.

He isn't Del Fontaine, thank God,
the French Canadian featherweight,
even though they could be twins.

Whose strangled girlfriend.
Double Windsor round her puckered neck.
Blue tongue. Squeezed out of its tube.

1937: *The Golden Bough*

Two sudden twigs of lightning.
The Alps in spats. Gone.
Kidnapped by thunder.

The tunnel into Germany
lit by electric sizzle
like a welder's arc.

Then Lydia lets fall
the corner of the blind,
and turns to the compartment:

the nightlight's glow
of bilberries in cream,
sleep, socks, suitcases, sprawl.

At 6, SS and customs officers
polite on the threshold:
eyes from photograph to face,

a few pages of passport turned,
returned, a croquet click of heels,
the Hitlergruss and gone.

No 'purpose of visit?' To visit.
No 'why this particular route?'
Better to come to München

from England via Switzerland
because better for a Jew.
A longer route, but less in Germany.

From these clapper-board heels,
cut. To Fedya's sitting room.
Action. Inaction. Silence.

Zhonya's face has hiccoughs.
Lydia looks at the piano stool,
its four bandy bulldog legs.

Lenchen's new nail scissors
trim off stiff eyelashes
on the doll that Tante brought.

Karlchen arranges Rowntree's Smarties,
a brand new English sweet.
Quarantined by colour.

The boy has chicken pox:
hard white blobs of candle grease,
windows of translucent fat,

suet crusts, cigarette burns,
craters, one of the damned
in some medieval frieze.

A whited sepulchre of calamine.
Pitted whitewash.
A firing squad wall.

Fedya, self-made man,
successful banker, Lutheran,
has requested Lydia

to confine her calls on them
until after dark. His tense hands.
The anger in his voice. At her.

We have to think of the children.
It's inconsiderate. We love you.
But your features look so Jewish.

Middle shot to mantelpiece:
an arachnid Indian goddess
bares her brassy breasts.

Juts her butt.
Saved from nigger decadence
by the kicking crosses,

swastikas around the base.
Dissolve to Lydia.
Her struggling face.

The Jewish mouth recites:
One fine day in the middle of the night,
Two dead men got up to fight . . .

The mouth recites:
Frusten war's: der Mond schien helle,
Schnee lag auf der grünen Flur,

Als ein Wagen blitzes schnelle
Langsam um die Ecke fuhr . . .
At least the children laugh.

Recites in Russian:
Рано утром вечерком
Поздно на рассвете...

Quatsch mit Sosse.
Nonsense in any language.
The lightning's genealogies.

1937: *England versus Germany*

Gnats flash, dazzle, disappear
on the asphalt outside the Albert Hall.
Then the rain stops. Rough diamonds.

The billboard in aspic announces:
England versus Germany.
I am the buzz of anticipation.

I am Pontius Pilate,
procurator, washing my hands
in the whole bloody business.

Box him. Box him. Tie him up.
Legs and feet. Legs and feet.
Left him. Left him. Dance and box.

I am Pilate, wishing my hands
in the whole bloody business.
Boxing is the noble art

of hitting without being hit.
Just out of reach,
the boxers face each other,

balanced on both feet equally,
the left from 10 to 20 inches
in front of the right.

In the red corner, Otto Kästner,
Olympic champion, oiled, tanned,
hair flighted like an arrow.

His broken-nosed opponent,
Norman Raine: white, visibly veined,
hair wavy as an Alsatian's palate.

Both are featherweights,
the middle of the order
because the English skipper,

a Cockney heavyweight, was scared:
begin with the flies
and finish up with the heavies.

But the flies and the bantams
want the fights to be fought
the other way round. Heavies to flies.

So Norman volunteers to start.
My Lords, Ladies and Gentlemen,
an alteration to your programme ...

In the red corner,
Marquess of Queensberry Rules.
In the blue, a *caestus*.

Which is not a *cestus*,
an item of ladies' lingerie.
One knocks you down. One stands you up.

The classical *caestus* is a thong
vertebraed with iron balls
like a broad bean

and wound around the fist.
Or sometimes studded with nails
like the husk of a chestnut.

Use your reach. Reach. Box him.
Jab. Jab. Feet and jab and.
The left foot is flat,

the right heel slightly raised.
The left side turned a fraction
to present the smallest target.

When the hands are clenched,
the thumb is doubled,
thus avoiding sprain,

behind the third and second fingers.
There are several dangerous blows:
to the solar plexus

and its network of nerves,
to the point of the chin,
impairing equilibrium . . .

Foul, ref, foul. Foul.
He's using his head. Foul.
Kästner has butted both Norman's eyes.

The lids begin to mizzle blood,
split and spirt. A broken fan.
The referee looks at Norman

looking through his eyelids
and is about to stop the fight
and Norman asks for the rest of the round.

Is not refused. Fight on.
Eurydamas swallowed his teeth
rather than show he was hurt.

And went on to win.
Give him the heel of the glove.
Jamming his left

underneath Kästner's armpit,
Norman pulls his opponent
between his right glove and the ref.

He's holding, ref.
And on the blind side,
gives Kästner the heel of the glove,

the lethal trellis of laces
ripped up and down his face
like a credit-card machine.

Through a gash darkly,
look at the red on his teeth.
Bright menstrual blood on porcelain.

Enough. From the back of beyond,
Raine wins on points,
wins by a foul.

1938: *The Company Car*

One hunchback robin hops. Hops.
Winds have rinsed the peppered may.
The silence of frontiers.

Sun and the stink of petrol.
A bee like a liquorice allsort.
Wayside flowers waiting to move,

still as a still photograph.
As Zhonya's passport photograph
which is causing the problem.

All eyes, taken in Moscow
at the time of the famine,
so starved her periods stopped,

it shows an older woman
than the one crossing her legs,
whsst, whssht, twenty years later,

in the back of this Opel Kadett
like someone posing for a photograph,
leather gloves asleep in her lap.

Furious, afraid, Fedya shivers
like water coming to the boil.
Zhonya looks straight ahead,

beyond the boom of the customs post,
to where the road evaporates.
The horizon's earthquake of heat.

Gestapo boots on the gravel,
as if fuming in acid,
tops accented grave and acute,

grit in the ear
like a faulty connection,
raised seams on the jodhpurs,

black leather glove
holding the passports.
A pace behind, the customs officer

in grey with dark green trim.
The black buffer hat
bends to the rear side window.

Patent peak. Insignia. Brown eyes.
'Heil Hitler. You can let them through.
She *is* Frau Pasternak.'

And to Fedya: 'Remember me?'
Before the Geheimestaatspolizei,
he used to drive a taxi.

'You always gave good tips.'
Years ago, when Fedya took taxis,
never the company car and chauffeur,

before this Jewish thing.
He wants a lift to Austria.
Three on the back seat,

a little squashed,
and Fedya falls asleep
while chauffeur and cabbie

debate the finer points
of bodywork and engine performance.
Better than the 5.8 litre Hansa.

Fedya's head lolls
on the officer's epaulette.
Spoke wheels and tiepin bumper.

Side indicators fold away
like cut-throat razors.
His glove on Zhonya's knee.

Fedya's mouth amazed in his sleep.
Headlamps behind their mesh.
Zhonya donating her knee.

Swing rear axle.
Independent front suspension.
A buzz eaten by distance.

1939: *Digging for England*

Fedya's finger screwing his ring.
Norman digging an air-raid shelter
in the back garden of Garden Square.

Sheathing the spade in England
like someone unsheathing a sword.
Or drawing the black-out. Whssht.

Whssht. And nggh. The costive sound
of a soul at stool. Nggh.
Whssht and nggh to a depth

of six feet, a boxing ring
of 15 feet six inches square.
Sweat leaving his shirt

heavily inked like a lino cut.
Two halves of a worm
squirming away from each other.

Fedya's radiant toecap,
studded with opals of dew,
turns out of its nest

an ancient tennis ball,
its sodden pith like a grated lemon.
A snail in its strapless décolletage.

The walls are the wooden walls
of the old garden shed.
Woozy for years. Easily swayed.

Earth steps, down one wall,
finished with apple-crate.
The roof topped off with turf.

Overgrown with undergrowth,
four mounds are cleared
on Mrs Pretty's estate.

Rabbits have left
dun rosaries of droppings.
'Why not start with this one?'

So an approach trench is laid
to the largest by Basil Brown,
the local archaeologist,

on 35 bob per week plus board.
Enthroned in a tub bedroom chair,
a Rose-du-Barry 'Lloyd Loom',

wickerwork frosted with gold,
Brown directs the gardeners,
Spooner and Jacobs,

who skim away the fallen roof
with ordinary coal shovels
on the end of very long handles

like paddles in a pizzeria.
The scabby hilt of a sword,
gold leaf on the wind,

coins like three-quarter moons,
and Phillips called in from Ipswich.
Brown takes a back seat to C. W.:

thin hair painted on his scalp
with very broad brushstrokes.
Shovels are set aside

for bodkins and bellows,
the badger-hair toothbrush.
At Woodbridge Station,

C. W. meets the London train
with a tobacco tin
containing a golden buckle,

salted with stones like a pretzel,
and shows it to the BM's Kendrick
on its moist bed of baccy.

Therefore the Office of Works
orders a mile of barbed wire,
tying itself in knots

and running around in circles.
The whssht of the bellows,
the nggl of bodkins. For months.

Until: the ship's outline
like a millipede's rictus
left by a wet bicycle tyre.

Two apostle spoons.
A nest of six silver bowls.
A two foot ceremonial whetstone.

The silver rims and mounts
of seven auroch drinking horns.
Wilf Grimes in his boiler suit,

C. W. P. in navyblue pinstripe,
and Olive in her apron,
packing the treasures in moss,

packing the moss into boxes,
pillboxes, chocolate boxes,
boxes of Meltis New Berry Fruits.

This warrior's moustached mask,
its rust bleeding in the rain,
makes her think of Norman

looking through his eyelids
like someone looking through a mask.
She'll marry him. In Oxford.

In Oxford, Zhonya is half an orphan.
Her mother dead of a heart attack.
A new language to learn,

the Anglo-Saxon tongue. Whssht.
Sky tadpoles trawling for flies.
War less than a week away.

1940: *Bergen Belsen*

The sound of trains at the railhead
like a saw panting through wood.
Phosphorescent in the dawn,

logs, a stack of birch logs,
loom on the tip of his tongue:
tinned pilchards in translation.

David Kroll, amazingly, smiles.
At roll-call yesterday evening,
the Dutch contingent's ragged shout:

Drei Liter. And not *Heil Hitler.*
Straightaway you couldn't be sure.
Because it seemed impossible.

Barbed wire like interference,
tearing up the postcard view.
Neatly. The German efficiency joke:

some benighted peasant touching nettles,
'Bloody Germans. Electric everywhere.'
Probably a Pole. Good for any language.

Kroll has acquired a spoon. A spoon.
He has already memorised its features.
He would recognise it anywhere.

Now he must find a hiding place.
Poe's 'Purloined Letter'.
Hide it with the other spoons.

Very funny. What other spoons?
Think, Kroll, think. *Think.*
He will hide it in the same place

it was hidden when he found it.
The owner won't look there again,
once he's looked and found it gone.

Seen it, seen his spoon,
and seen her vanish as he looked.
The infidelity of spoons.

And human greed. That poor sod
six months ago, just arrived,
telling his little girl

how everything began: when clothes
were handed out to all the animals,
the monkey and the cat were greedy

and grabbed the first things they saw.
Which is why the cat has four socks
and the monkey has two pairs of gloves.

Then he had a heart attack.
Unforgettable, his masturbator's mask.
Horsey, said the kid, astride his corpse.

Father and four year old daughter,
matching rings under their eyes.
The colour of paper

about to burst into flames.
What is the reason for that,
the physiological reason?

Zolya could probably say.
(His wife, the doctor at Vitel,
a camp for foreign nationals,

less vivid than a spoon,
and quite unable to explain
because the reason is not known.

There is no reason to know.)
Whereas boiled flies
provide a source of protein.

Whereas the starving lie down
because it uses energy to stand.
As Kroll does now. Battlefield effect.

Though when the picket comes
he clambers to his feet at once.
The Commandant? Why?

The reason is not known.
That margarine paper he stole,
the headache of each lick? The spoon?

You face the Commandant's face,
the scar on his cheek like a gill,
those lashless bull-terrier eyes,

crimson with conjunctivitis,
because your daughter has worked,
lobbied MPs, the Swedish ambassador,

paid 50,000 Reichsmark in bribes,
to have you translated to Wülzburg,
another camp for foreign nationals.

Here is your railway warrant,
Nansen passport, civilian clothes.
Your daughter remembers you both

by remembering how you dressed.
She starts at your shoes
and works up to your faces.

She has an eye for clothes,
she buys for Simpson's, Piccadilly.
All night, before tomorrow,

David worries and wonders
whether to save the spoon
or leave it in this factory of breath.

1940: *Ja bin die Papi's Spoek*

Suddenly over your eyes from behind,
Vsevolod Meyerhold's bony hands
and that comic Afrikaans:

Omlet, Omlet, ja bin die Papi's Spoek.
So you always knew it was him.
Right shoulder higher than the other,

bow tie, horn-rims, brittle hair,
long upper lip, barrel-stave teeth,
a micro-climate of eau de cologne,

rapid tight-rope walker's walk,
and, of course, obsessed by *Hamlet.*
He lives in Borya's head,

unprotected, indiscreet, a gas,
describing Chaplin at Versailles,
the grey-haired, suited gravitas

suddenly changing to Charlie,
a minor miracle to please the crowd.
'The classics must live so.'

Borya's *Hamlet* at the Writers' Club,
read now by the author,
owes everything to Meyerhold,

onlie begetter and up-dater,
director not a bloody archaeologist,
dispenser of the proscenium arch.

Boris renders Shakespeare's page,
escapes the tyranny of word for word,
takes liberties. Deliberately.

The credo might be Meyerhold's.
Who planned a pair of actors
in the part: one bold,

one indecisive, alternating
in the same performance.
You have to bring the thing to life.

And yet he never did the piece,
but lived up to his jokey epitaph:
Here lies V. E. Meyerhold, Director,

Who Never Directed *Hamlet* Once.
He is dead and gone, lady.
And also Zinaida, Wife of the Above,

who was murdered at home,
three weeks after his arrest.
Borya, like everyone, is baffled,

stops in the middle of a line
to wonder what happened,
caesura sliding into silence.

Sliding into total silence.
Put you out of your misery?
I was there on both occasions.

Protesting. Buzzing the actors.
Naturally enough. I'm bloody-minded.
No question, I can be bloody-minded.

What happened was this:
bio-mechanics at the Lubianka,
a limited range of gestures.

They began by breaking his spectacles
and he began to be scared.
After this oddly effective first act,

they broke his left hand.
It was rather a scream.
The bare minimum of dialogue.

Unwilling suspension of disbelief.
Spot-lit, a ghost without his specs,
vague, pale as distemper,

except for the definite umlaut
red on his nose,
he signed the document, V. E. Meyerhold.

It took him almost two hours,
his signature's electroencephalograph.
Left-handed. Apart from anything else.

He implicated everyone.
He implicated everyone.
In triplicated everyone.

And she? The wife? Zinaida Raikh?
They put her eyes out, first.
She only answered the door,

as it happened, to no one she knew.
They pressed the bell continuously.
Who's there? They pressed the bell.

It was 10 past three in the morning.
And then she thought she heard
Ja bin die Papi's Spoek.

It was hard to tell.
She drew the bolts, top and bottom.
Four total strangers stood outside,

one a woman, pressing the bell.
She couldn't see their faces.
'We come from Vsevolod Emilyevich.'

Cheka. 'Won't you please come in?'
Actress, she turned in her kimono,
buttocks slowly chewing the cud,

and never reached the drawing room.
Fingers over her eyes. Pressing the bell.
She could feel his cock grow hard.

Gat-toothed, Borya stands aghast,
adrift, alone on the bare stage.
And is saved by Tsvetayeva,

arrested in the doorway, late,
without Efron, without Ariadna,
grey, ghastly, ghostly, all alone.

Borya leaves the stage,
takes her hand and kisses it,
leads her to a front row seat.

1940: *Various Preservatives*

Pale cherries bottled in blood,
an igloo of eggs, upside-down
in isinglass, submarine plums,

kitchen windows crossed out
with union jacks of sticky tape,
sandbags sheltering against the walls,

and Rudi Mendelssohn, the father,
with Rudi Mendelssohn, the son,
sitting in the basement kitchen

where the daughter used to work.
Newly shipped from Germany
under the Panamanian flag.

From Dachau to Harwich to Oxford,
via Nürnberg, Würzburg, Aschaffenburg,
Frankfurt, Osnabrück, Emden,

to attend the inquest in Putney
and identify her frozen corpse.
A kept woman. Waiting for weeks.

Her nose was broken off
like a classical statue.
She was furry with frost,

looked blind from both eyes.
Lydia asks about Dachau.
There are two camps, not one.

Induction and the main camp.
The first a disinfection station:
they take away your clothes,

supply fumigated camp pyjamas,
clipper off all body hair,
inject against typhus,

one needle per 50 inmates.
In the main camp everyone works,
but everybody wants to go there.

Why? He rubs his bristly head.
The lavatories are clean.
Washrooms too. Headed Dachau notepaper.

Now he asks about Erna.
Impossible to tell the truth.
Couldn't trust her with children.

Lydia offers an egg instead.
Bruised pastel plush yolk.
Says: I found her difficult.

She stuck hats with hat-pins
on my father's portrait paintings.
Made mistakes in her English:

getting down to brass taps.
Lydia can't translate the joke.
We got on badly. She left for London.

Mendelssohn tells the table-top:
she went to Mrs Brookes's bedroom
naked one night. Gar nichts.

She tried to get into bed.
Twice. Both sides. In total silence.
One side, then the other. No.

She lay down on the floorboards.
Five minutes. Dressed. Disappeared.
Next day, dinner at the Dorchester,

then jumped off Putney Bridge.
The railway bridge. A ringweight,
20 lb, tied round her neck.

He looks at Lydia now. And laughs.
For us, it is lucky. A lucky escape.
Two fingers shoot his temple.

Knock-kneed ungainly ghost.
Caught against the curtain.
Body hair: spiders round each nipple.

Her groin, her armpits:
the black blaze of dead fires,
dark holocausts of hair.

1940: *Christmas Day in Bed*

Eliot and Jeanie have been playing
doctors and nurses most of the night
in Will and Mary Sargant's empty flat.

After Chaplin as *The Great Dictator*,
Adenoid Hynkel, the secret Jew,
Dr Raine and staff nurse Fyfe

walked back through the black-out
towards their theoretical desire
and the Sargants' Siamese cat

with its oiled black ears
like the tips of chicory
left in walnut oil. Pre-war.

Her high heels prattled,
answered to his weightier brogues,
flirted with falling in step.

Eliot would prefer to eat her pussy,
would like to pull it apart
and get at the guava, juices

tart on the tip of his tongue.
He would like to tell her this,
wallowing in 'cunt', the word.

Instead, a longish walk to Bayswater,
discussing Chaplin's didactic strain
and its diametric opposite,

the suddenly terpsichorean tyrant,
whose balletic grace and balance
are meant to show the opposite,

a crank, the balance of whose mind . . .
You almost wonder what side he's on.
Silence. Talking of which.

The balance, Eliot means.
Drawing on his briar, Dr Raine,
confides, aposiopetically,

a case, history, of, interest,
to, a colleague. A corporal in the RAF.
Demented after Dunkirk. Mania.

Obsessed with abbreviations.
BEF, e.g. Or DPM, camouflage,
Disruptive Pattern Marking.

Anyway. (Why, thinks Eliot,
rationing his phrases,
weighing his words, professional,

arranging the stem of his pipe,
this amorous austerity?
I want your *Liebensraum.*)

The fucking British army
beat him fucking senseless
in some fucking sand dunes

they were fucking sheltering in,
because their fucking regiment,
or what was fucking left of it,

came under fucking friendly fire
from a fucking Spitfire,
and the fucking cry went up:

the RA fucking F. The RA fucking F.
You fucking little sod.
You little sodding fucker.

The RAF in strafe. The marram
flattened like flame under a saucepan.
Low. A flying Singer sewing machine

firing a double seam of shells.
In stitches. The CSM's teeth
all over his face. Pissing himself.

Fists for hours on end. And belts.
The corporal's face soft fruit.
Spoiled fruit. Torn fruit. Jam.

At night he finds it hard to sleep,
feeling the force field again:
foreshortened, furious features

crammed up against his own.
And so he needed morphine,
broke into the poison cupboard,

took between five and seven grains,
and survived unscathed. Unscathed.
He woke up in the morning.

Eliot brains his briar on his brogue
and feels for the key. At last,
the Sargants' basement flat,

where it isn't worth lighting a fire.
Cocoa substitute? *Camp?* Tea?
(Tea ration forethoughtfully to hand.)

They keep their coats on,
smile at the kettle like a patient,
and chat about the Kaiser,

still alive, at Scheveningen,
watching the North Sea mixing cement,
in his invalid carriage,

legs in the black rubber sheath
like a merman, talons on the T-bar,
turning his back to the Nazi invasion.

We should be in each other's arms,
instead of talking all this tripe,
thinks Eliot. Beauty on the bed.

On a pillow, Sargant's note,
superscribed to Eliot Raine, Esquire,
in steel-nibbed copperplate,

already fading blue-black flourishes:
Pray feed the animal.
Provender within the meat safe.

Mithras be with you.
Enjoy a happy Saturnalia.
To't, Luxury, pell-mell. Will.

How can they enjoy themselves
in front of all this furniture,
the upright audience

of dining room chairs,
the buttoned-up sofa
on its best behaviour,

knick-knacks and props
in some Victorian period piece?
Acting the part,

they brush their teeth,
wash in cold water,
taking turns in the bathroom.

Paired in pyjamas,
they crawl between cold sheets.
Passionless peppermint breath.

His fingers on her breast
shocking as a stethoscope.
The only human touch

a groaning, intermittent ghost
somewhere in his bowel's oubliette.
He rubs her right hip

like a radiator, risks
a gynaecological caress.
Squeaky intercourse concludes

with coitus interruptus.
Then folded like a frozen fly.
But in the middle of the night . . .

All the same, all the same,
leaving Jean, he feels the same
as leaving Lydia. A huge relief.

1941: *Mawcarse*

Let me try to put you in the picture.
Action painting. What a bally mess.
How best to piece things together?

We could start with a definition.
How do you define a Scotsman?
A Geordie with his brains bashed out.

We could search for the dead
by the light of our cigarettes.
One of the injured is smoking a fag

but something is seriously wrong.
He exhales smoke from everywhere
except his mouth, like a Turkish bath.

Love moans come from the wounded.
The whole of his battledress top
is oozing fog like a freezer.

I should explain where we are.
Mawcarse is an RAF bomb dump
in a guarded pine wood.

Smashed, it smells of disinfectant.
Bunting, bits of battledress,
branches fluttering with flesh.

Peaceful as a Shinto shrine.
Where were we now?
Between Kinross and Milnathort.

I could say who I am:
that trickling sensation,
which might be blood. Or sweat.

Or tears. Or something else.
Last night, tonight, was Hogmanay,
and the squad got wrecked.

Legless. Bombed. Out of their skulls.
Which is why Norman looks pissed,
soused enough to be singing,

O tell me the truth, mother,
tell me the truth,
do kippers swim folded or flat?

Cross-eyed, unable to focus,
black tongue, fuddled feet;
tomorrow he'll be on a fizzer.

They'll charge him with malingering,
with bloody Munchausen's, because
he isn't bleeding from the ears.

He has a triple-fractured skull,
internal bleeding, and, in days,
acute subserous meningitis.

He's awa in the heid. Wandering.
Down by the stream. Bird song.
All the willows washing their hair.

The perfect plumage of pine cones.
A threadbare spider's web. Fucked.
Big black cock in his kisser.

Oot on it. Completely fucked.
In 28 days, he'll forget the lot:
falling out of the jeep,

two field hospital operations,
let alone his letter to Olive
from sick quarters in camp.

'Head injured by a piece of coal.'
His handwriting. Signed it 'Geordie'.
He hasn't the faintest idea.

1941: *Professor Dot*

A blackbird chiselling granite.
Dawn at the Edinburgh Royal.
Norman is lying awake,

the wince of sound in his ears,
his shaven head on the pillow,
seamed like a hot cross bun.

He is thinking things through,
Professor Dot's latest prognosis.
Yesterday morning. The big chief,

talking to Dr Watt,
toying with a book of matches
like a Red Indian headdress.

As Norman raised two knuckles
to rap backhanded on the open door,
he heard dispassionate discussion.

What are Raine's actual chances,
now he has had the first fit?
His hand, double-stopped, in mid air

like a fiddler's fingering. Wait.
Eighteen months at the very outside.
As little as that? How will he go?

Without knocking, Norman interrupts:
Good question. How *will* I go?
Professor Dot is displeased.

The cube of ash on his cigar
is contemplated and brushed off.
Perfect co-ordination.

Not eavesdropping, are we? he asks,
lugging his left leg on its pedestal
as he crosses to close the door.

Every step he takes
like a clockwork cowboy
trying to mount. On his high horse.

Norman: I was going to knock.
But the door was wide open.
Silent, these rubber-soled . . .

And Dot: Well, you may as well know.
I diagnose a slow deterioration
in the brain's left hemisphere.

Your right side will get paralysed.
Then I'd predict a rapid decline.
Blindness. Possible madness. Death.

Eighteen months. As I said.
Tell me, what do you remember, Raine?
Give us some idea. Anything at all?

The runway at RAF Leuchars
like a squash court with skids.
Landing lights in a line

like pins in a tailor's lapel.
To det 4,000 pounders,
you needed three tapes up.

Fully detted bombs
had detonators nose and tail
and all along their length.

Sunk in sponge rubber. Prophylactic.
Anything could bring them off.
Winched straight into the bomb bays.

When you sawed the top off my skull,
the pressure I felt. Not pain.
The pong of burning bone.

The hesitant, crumbling buzz
of surgical brace and bit. Stopping.
Hardly anything at all, he says.

1941: *The Gorbals*

Norman and Robert McGregor:
A. C. Plonks, the only two
recuperating at Gleneagles Hotel.

All the rest are officers.
Longest way up,
shortest way down. Quick march.

Give the saluting a rest, old thing.
Red-eyed in the rhododendrons.
Weepy with stress. By the dozen.

Which means the airmen
get a bathroom to themselves.
Other Ranks, for the ablutions of.

The cold tap's icicle,
the hot tap's dry uncontrollable cough.
A caddy of toothbrushes.

But McGregor brushes his teeth
by lighting a fag,
washes by combing his hair

with water out of the hot.
Yet, perfect teeth, white,
and odourless armpits.

McGregor, in front of the mirror,
expelling a fart with a frown.
Get out and walk. Severe.

Norman feels his new hair
for the holes in his skull.
A shamrock of inners. Another.

They are going to Glasgow,
to McGregor's home in the Gorbals,
on a weekend pass, in hospital blues.

But his new address
has somehow gone into hiding.
He has to ask where he lives,

where the house-warming is.
Door to door, like detectives.
Whisht. Dinna say that. OK?

In the stone tenement hallway,
a dark continent of urine
and the McGregor coat of arms:

a long cock and balls,
in chalk, like a DDT spray.
Now he minds where it is.

Mrs McGregor bursts into tears.
Or bursts out laughing. Or both.
She has taken a drop. Aye, a drop taken.

After the Gleneagles Hotel,
the glaze of T'ang vases
(dusky duplicates sunk

in rosewood surfaces),
Persian rugs on parquet floors,
dimpled Chesterfield sofas,

this limbo of smoke,
of uncarpeted concrete.
Mrs McGregor is sick in the sink.

Like a beer pump. Twice.
Burps. Lights up a nip. Exhales.
Feela bit billiards.

The seatless, waterless w.c.
is set over a cesspit outside,
down two stone flights.

The T'ang of ammonia
from an underworld of excrement.
The bottomless pit.

Furry with grey fly,
the porcelain bowl, stirring.
Like a shaven armpit.

Diz Norman wanni diman ring?
Fo fefteen boab? Wonni thes?
Solitaire clasped like a cauliflower.

They're not hot, are they?
Dinner be sane that. O K?
Everyone's listening. Everyone.

So bring over Benny Lynch,
his yarmulka of baldness,
Tolstoy's thermometer nose.

Annitha wannyi boaxas, Benny.
(Ex-flyweight champion of the world,
bobbing and weaving,

punch drunk or plain drunk,
broke as his nose:
longest way up, shortest way down.)

Wass sure nem, Jimmy?
Norman Raine. Knobser Raine.
Herder ewe. Herder ewe. Bias her drink.

And in the *Mirror* on Monday:
GLASGOW JEWELLER MURDERED.
Dinner breathe a wurd. OK?

Or yirra ded man. Snow joke.
Yi can haud awa till Egypt,
disguise sell find use. Terra.

Nigh forra nigh. Justice.
How do you plead? Human.
For mercy, forgiveness.

Norman is flaming well guilty.
Her name is Elaine
and she works in the kitchens.

Her joke about Hughie McEwan:
garbled Gorbals for Menuhin.
It was innocent, perfect,

till she brought him round
after 15 three-minute fits,
touched off by Technicolor

when they went to the pictures.
An arsehole of lipstick
blotted on Bronco. Pictures.

He hasn't seen Olive since Christmas.
Eight months. Where does he live?
Red-eyed in the rhododendrons. Both.

1941: *Fire-watching*

Bombers above and the braille of stars.
Twelve storeys down, the dusty street,
blind in the black-out.

A humid September night, searchlights,
dutiful Boris out on the tiles,
in shirtsleeves, armband, soup plate.

At the far end of Lavrushensky,
an apartment block eviscerates,
hit by four or five incendiaries.

Sturm und Drang. Coup de foudre.
Twisting its galvanised windows,
breaking china, breaking glass,

tearing itself apart, baring
its soul, on fire like Hercules.
Or like Tsvetayeva in love.

Who was the torch she carried,
who taught poetry the torch song.
Her Joan of Arc: 'the pyre is mine.

Theirs the transcript of the trial.'
Filing clerk and firebrand,
setting fire to herself,

always surviving this art of scars.
Until something was broken down.
The transcript of her trials?

Call Boris Leonidovich Pasternak.
Buzz. Buzz. Silence in court.
How does the witness plead?

Guilty. Guilty before God.
(Boris has found out from Fedin
about her suicide in Elabuga.)

She told me when we said goodbye
at Khimki River port
that she was looking for a hook

and had been looking for a year,
since her return to Russia,
paraffin, dishwater, and paranoia.

Sunshine squiggled on the water.
I felt that she was talking for effect.
It sounded written. Something for a poem.

I told her to look for food instead.
They had nothing for the journey.
She thought the boat would have a buffet.

One suitcase full of loose cigarettes.
We can always smoke for breakfast.
She bought two open sandwiches

and waved her silver bangles.
Goodbye. They shone like irons.
I saw the wash. It came and kissed

the wharf and travelled on.
I felt relieved to watch the boat
go round the bend. Low in the water.

She was dangerous to know
and hard to help. Still arrogant,
after three months in a cupboard,

sleeping on a trunk. We sat
on Peredelkino Station platform,
talking poetry, rhyme schemes, scansion,

ignoring all the trains to Moscow.
She, oblivious. And I?
I was frightened she would miss the last.

Zina wouldn't have her in the house.
Now she lodges in my conscience,
still taking five days

to polish up some hack translation,
twenty lines of poetry
I'd knock off in a morning.

She couldn't compromise.
I begged her not to go to Elabuga
but was glad when she went

to save her son from bomb disposal.
The worthless Mur. His bitten nails,
the taint of gouda on his fingers.

Telling her how old she looked.
True. When she smiled, her teeth
were like an X-ray of teeth.

A deep, dirty, circular seam
ran right under her chin
from nostril wing to nostril wing,

like a ventriloquist's dummy.
The skin was orange peel.
Under the eyebrows, unironed.

Caught without her spectacles,
she shied away from books,
held literature at arm's length.

Skin tags like tonsils, milts.
Ankle socks. Her knitted beret
like the halo on a toffee apple.

Thin, but thick in the waist.
The puckered cleavage.
Still she bore herself

as if she were a beauty.
Cream cheese impasto
with radishes and gherkins, chopped.

Her last words to Borya were:
I am already dead. Have been for months.
One cassata sandwich. Want a bite?

Exactly twenty-one days later,
Tsvetayeva had found the hook
and hanged herself. Not because

she had failed to get a job
as dishwasher in the writers' canteen.
(Too many other applicants.)

Because, in Chistopol, three people,
Misha and Tania Schneider,
Lydia Chukovskaya, had taken pity.

It was a touch of warmth
in which she burned alive,
A Woman Killed with Kindness.

Wood, thinks fire-watching Borya,
solid, reliable, and suicidal.
Ruins chainsmoke like Tsvetayeva.

1941: *Blitz*

Haunted by *Blithe Spirit* still,
thinking of Jeanie's thorn-shaped navel,
her russet pubic goatee, the Blitz,

and Lydia's discovery of his diaries,
Eliot peers into the black-out
over his Hillman's steering wheel.

Though better than the two-inch hole
and single stem of light
laid down in earlier regulations

(a waste of wartime cardboard),
the single headlamp's brief bouquet
is glaringly inadequate.

And streets keep disappearing.
You turn right or left into rubble.
Trial and error. Cliffhanger Street.

You need to be clairvoyant.
Sometimes you are clairvoyant
and see, *plein air*, a porcelain hippo,

ascending into heaven,
the mixer tap's top brass
and its trachea of braid.

Or a first-floor drawing room
like a raft tilting over a waterfall,
poised with furniture

and perfect with Persian rugs
Pity about the incontinent pipes.
Shame the fireplace shat itself.

And now the sirens start
like Munch's woodcut of *Der Schrei*
(82 degenerate works seized in 1937).

When the windscreen shatters,
Eliot pulls over to the curb,
and says they should enjoy the show.

So shitstruck he forgets
the cowering helmet under his seat.
He thinks of Regensburg,

and a fountain's faint ghost,
naked, bruised by a rainbow.
But the shock of the bombs

brings him the shock in Lydia's voice.
Why am I poked? Why am I poked?
Eliot could hear the Singer

tapping its foot, somewhere upstairs.
And then full blast: I asked you
a question. Why am I poked?

It says so here. 'Poked L.' Thanks.
(Not this current year, thank God.)
Why are your other ones 'rogered'?

Why can't I be rogered or trevored?
Lydia's tearful attempt at a joke
like the wailing All-Clear.

Eliot covers his eyes,
discovers wet on his cheek.
Superficial cut to his scalp,

requiring a couple of stitches,
3,000 units of ATS by injection,
so over London Bridge to Guy's.

Where Eliot is known. But not Lydia.
So everyone assumes that Jeanie . . .
Very nice to meet you, Mrs Raine.

No contradiction. No going back.
Bombarded by greetings, by light.
Outside, night dark as chocolate.

In the dispensary office,
Izzard explains Wittgenstein:
famous philosopher from Cambridge

that no one has heard of,
hiding behind an alias here,
job as dispensary porter,

there, with the arachnoid eyebrows,
arrogant sod, excuse my French,
tried to show me how the unit should run.

(Plunges the needle into the phial.)
And he won't let the other chaps whistle.
I cannot tolerate these musical mistakes;

it is too painful; kindly stop. Egotist.
He can whistle a bloody Brandenburg,
Beethoven's Pastoral, Schubert's Unfinished.

(The hypodermic's premature ejaculate.)
That should do the job OK.
And you. Bye bye. Take care. Take care.

Back in the car, Eliot dons his helmet.
Doesn't even offer it to Jeanie.
Drops her at the Nurses' Home.

1941: *Chistopol*

Outside, minus 30. Twice today,
annunciations. Leafleted by snow.
Puddles cracked like cranefly wings.

Inside the writers' cafeteria,
Brrrrya's talcum breath,
his English–Russian dictionary,

his *Romeo and Juliet*,
his woollen, fingerless gloves,
the numb, fingerless fingers,

and what Akhmatova now designates
'the almost unbelievable luxury'
of granulated sugar in a bowl

(true, the bowl is missing a chip
and complete with brown bogey).
A recent refugee from Leningrad,

she remembers going to a shop,
an expensive place by the Hermitage,
to buy in for the siege,

six days before the Germans came.
Too late, of course, but six days
felt two years away. Oddly relaxed.

Borya observes her heavy breathing,
the sudden snag of her thread,
the way her needle picks

at the huddled spider.
No flour, no salt, no bread.
They had caviar and almonds.

Which she therefore bought.
And ate before the blockade began.
Then starved. And starved.

Until (eyes searching the ceiling,
voice arrested, hand to mouth)
she ate the prison parcels

set aside for forwarding to Lev,
via the window at Kresty,
on the Vyborg side of Leningrad.

To God knows where. Glazed with tears.
(Lev Nikolayevich, the son,
who was once her child,

green bruises on his shins
like a new potato.
My God, just think, thinks Borya,

a new potato. A new potato.)
Tactfully, he turns to Shakespeare,
'to remove that siege of grief from her'.

A tang of tango from the kitchens.
Deep, silent road outside.
The double windows dim,

shuttered tight with snow.
He finds his place. Back to IV Sc. i.
'Or shut me nightly in a charnel house.'

The doctors were butchers,
a source of suspect salami.
Night soil was disposed of hot

before it froze to bronze,
needing to be chiselled free.
Borya studies his new *valenki*.

White felt. Unusual and elegant.
He has heard all this before.
Needle-eyed at her needle eye,

Anna Arkadyevna Gorenko
squints, re-threads, begins again:
she lay in bed all day

and fantasised foam baths,
scented, hot and rustling.
From which she rose, a poodle.

Borya would like to change the record.
He opens the door to the kitchen –
for warmth, for the noise,

for a glimpse of women dancing,
breast to sloping breast. Appetite.
Feeling feeds his fingertips.

What did she think of Kostya
doing Gorky's Nizhny Novgorod twang,
his 'borrowed likeness of shrunk death'?

1942: *Trembling*

A temple to Mithras
discovered by bombing in London;
items of seventeenth-century armour,

salades, taces, tassets, sollerets,
discovered in the River Ray
from the Battle of Islip;

and Norman in hospital blues,
on Dover tablets
and using two sticks

to walk from Garden Square
up to St Hugh's, a patient
under Professor Hugh Cairns.

The college is requisitioned:
a hospital for injuries of the head.
Do not ask him how he is.

He will start to tremble.
His lower lip will start to tremble.
Where it feels for support,

his left hand will tremble
in the pot-pourri of paint
flaked onto the windowsill.

Black-outs more often these days.
One side of his head is shaven.
A dressing of paraffin gauze

protects his skull and scalp
from the chafe of his airman's hat.
They have put in a silver plate.

Shudders like the buck of sperm.
And stops. Eliot has seen him
but failed to explain it to Olive.

Attractive girl, by the bye.
His study of occupational therapy
takes St Hugh's as a test case.

Should be occupational therapies:
Rickman is administrative head
and hated by all the housemen.

When he comes into the Common Room,
they inspect their shoes for shit,
they drown his conversation

by turning up the wireless set.
Last week, a general came to lunch.
When Rickman filled his glass,

twenty housemen at the table
passed their glasses down as well.
Nice enough chap. But no control.

When he turns the wireless down,
they gather round the set
and use their stethoscopes.

Decidedly attractive girl.
A good pair of tits
when she suckles her son.

White and gold in Garden Square,
Mrs Pearson's papal flag
celebrates each allied conquest.

Brotherly love. Stitches like flies.
And the moon like Tom Rakewell
out of his baldy in Bedlam.

1942: *Arresting Ike*

In charge of Torch, of Gymnast,
of Bolero-Roundup-Gymnast,
of everything from soup to nuts,

General Dwight D. Eisenhower,
so kiss his stern, OK?,
you surly Scottish so-and-so's.

Tunnel time is 9 p.m.,
Gib time is 8, an hour earlier,
and Jimmy Raine is guarding the rock.

He has shaved his moustache,
tired of being teased
for looking like Hitler.

A low pyramid of pallor
on his upper lip. One stripe up,
4th Battalion Black Watch,

an outfit in disgrace,
posted to Gib as a punishment
because they cut and ran,

funk and disorderly,
instead of a strategic retreat
to the dunes of Dunkirk.

All day, sunlight has divided
like cells on the sea, and gone.
The full Mediterranean moon

is brighter than a microscope.
Still in civvies for security,
in case his plane was downed,

said to be in Washington,
Ike has been to pat the apes,
for luck, with Captain Butcher,

and Private Kronke, his driver.
South of the old Moorish wall,
the lavatorial lope

of the famous Barbary apes,
limbs like lianas,
showing their tonsured rumps,

cushions of callous,
vulvas like strangled inner tube.
Cracking fleas

in teeth like bitten fingernails.
When: who the fuck goes there?
Jimmy Raine on sentry go, seeing

some jerk in a jerkin and chinos.
And then two more in the dusk.
So he looses a round over their heads,

and the Supreme Commander
surrenders like a Morris man,
waving two white hankies aloft.

So scared, I could've fucked his arse,
says Jimmy later, in the mess.
Aye, I knew it was Donald Duck,

but I wanted the arrest to be logged.
First, the guardroom's regatta of glass,
and then the regiment's deepest regret. Aye.

1943: *Orel*

One of six with a military mission,
Boris is filling his notebook
on Turgenev's Spasskoye estate:

buds tight in puttees,
trout breathe like tweezers,
a squirrel shudders up a pine.

Tines of sunlight through the trees,
where Ivanov and Azarch
are looking for mushrooms,

downcast, with folded arms,
and wet, inquisitive toecaps.
So. A giant puffball, solid,

slick with dew, resilient,
texture like touching a dolphin.
Delicious. Already Simonov

is fixing a wigwam of fire.
Lard. Salt. Unfold the frying pan.
And look. A lizard like bellows.

The zip of its tongue
taking a gnat and a gnat
from the dodgem of gnats.

The waiting Dodge will take them
back to the front at Orel,
but first they will eat,

and Borya will walk on tiptoe,
crucified, up to his waist
in the black, icy river.

Then he'll slide in stocking feet
from room to room to room
across the woven, wooden floors,

while Serafimovich laughs
at the literary sacrilege,
throwing back his big, bald head,

the polished tan of a pomegranate.
Woooh! and another niente ending.
The length of the semicircular building.

This is the life. Woooh! Woooh!
Whereas Orel . . .
A corpse like a chorister,

eyes filled with dirt,
ack-ack like valerian drops
in a glass of water,

artillery raising a row of poplars,
garbled houses, cardboard coffins,
or that funnel-shaped ditch

where the dead were packed
like a barrel of herrings.
The lowest welded by weight.

The ground buckled by gas.
Rippled with stench. Borya prefers
this moth with brazier eyes,

frogspawn's filthy ermine,
its sexual slime to heavy transports
cutting Cyrillic into the fields.

1943: *Tram*

The nervous, dusty doors of the tram
open and slap shut like an umbrella,
admitting Borya and Gladkov,

who take the two steep steps,
gripping the steel stangs. Hup.
Opaque windows like greaseproof paper.

Full. All the wooden aertex seats
are taken. Standing room only.
Smells like a kitchen, of sweat.

Cigarettes crushed flat, Turkish,
grease-paints on the cleated floor.
Every armpit a sodden salt mine.

An old woman opens her bag
for a bottle of smelling salts.
Clears her head. Pickled diamonds.

While they corner, Gladkov whispers:
he has recently heard from his brother . . .
Boris's latest book received . . .

Drift lost in the railing of rails.
Deliberately. Because they don't exist,
it is dangerous to discuss the camps.

The gamboge tram corrects itself.
Jolting. Indignant metal. Roils.
Righting approximate cubist curves.

Borya waits for the row to subside.
Then, at the top of his voice:
your brother in the camp at Kolyma?

To think of Anton reading my stuff.
(An acrid asterisk of bluebottle,
the frazzle of overhead poles.)

I have another friend, he says,
who has an ironed handkerchief.
When things get bad, he looks at it.

The clean weave keeps him sane.
Civilisation. When you live in a latrine . . .
Everyone is listening. Everyone.

But what power has poetry against . . . ?
Borya leaves his question levitating.
Against the permafrost, he thinks.

Against the grind, the beach like liver,
against the black mosquito storms,
against the heaps of seaweed,

for use as fertiliser, effervescent,
stinking of stale sex,
stacked by connoisseurs of poetry.

His talking has emptied the tram
but continues to the terminus.
Borya, dead and buried,

like a clam's powder compact,
open, sandy, mirrorless.
Rescued by the terrified turntable.

1944: *My Poor Fool*

What became of Walde? Walde?
Poor Walde. Asked to plead,
at first he couldn't speak,

hair suddenly seeded with sweat
where it thinned at the temples.
His knee trembled in one trouser leg.

(How now! A rat? Up a drainpipe,
according to the WPC,
the one who made the arrest.)

His lips were sealed,
by a thin red line
of rubber solution,

stickily blackening, blackening.
The pool of wrinkles
deepened on his forehead

as he fought to speak, to speak,
to speak the unspeakable. Guilty.
Walde had said he was innocent

(well, not guilty as charged;
what he did do was bad enough)
but the case had brought on his shingles.

He had been tight on the tube,
playing footsie and egged on
by the smiling woman opposite.

Or: from Chalk Farm to Hampstead,
hiding behind his attaché case,
the accused took out his penis

and masturbated in full view.
Mlud? In my full view,
shielded from the other passengers.

I could see the accused was circumcised.
At Hampstead, we took the lift,
and the accused was given in charge

to a uniformed constable there.
(Waiting. Conveniently loitering
hard by the conveniences.)

The character witness for Walde
was Dr Eliot Raine, psychiatrist.
Has known Herr Walde seven years.

Jewish refugee. Gifted teacher.
First offence. Court appearance
perhaps sufficient punishment.

Momentary aberration. Post at risk.
Fined £15. £4 down.
Seven days to find the rest.

So, outside, Eliot signed a cheque,
post-dated, for eleven quid.
Pity you're not a pederast, Walde:

flies to your wanton boys, eh?
Much better bet. Cheer up, Walde.
It's not the end of the world.

And they wrangled (*sotto voce*)
in Lyons about *Lady Chatterley*,
Eliot's only contraband copy

which Walde had not returned.
Except that he had. And, for him,
it was the end of the world.

One night, taking a cut
through the university parks,
Norman walked into Walde's shoes.

Ouch. Head to toe. Pure coincidence.
A left and a right upstairs.
Knock knockout. Who's there?

A pair of semi-brogues,
clicking their heels,
cooling their tan willow heels,

belonging to Walde,
chin on his chest,
looking askance, black looks,

looking down his nose at Norman.
At the end of his tether.
Highly strung.

All of which Eliot recalls
when he discovers his mouth is dry
and *Le Doctorat Impromptu*

has disappeared from his desk.
But for a bit of fluff,
the deed box is bare.

Panic and emptiness.
His tongue, his cheeks, are suede.
His heart bumps and grinds.

Fear fetches up the perfect excuse:
part of his professional work
on sado-masochism. Psychopathology.

Spanking. Colonic irrigation. Bondage.
This, though, will scarcely explain
Eliot's own original stories,

six, pornographic, hand-written,
which have also been swiped.
They could be copies. Invent authors.

Were they signed? Or unsigned? Shit.
Crucial and he cannot remember.
Why did he leave it unlocked?

Might as well have cut his throat.
And then the General, poor sod,
returns from twenty years ago.

I am dying, idiot, dying.
Eliot was leaning with Norman
out of the first-floor window,

like yachtsmen, so they could see
into the summerhouse next door,
which belonged to the General.

A single pane
that wasn't frosted glass
showed a trunkful of erotica.

We stole the lot:
Illustrierte Sittengeschichte
von Eduard Fuchs, with artistic etchings

of 'Das Klystier', 'Das Strumpfband',
'Ohne Scham' by Félicien Rops;
The Culture of the Nude in China,

with 32 original photographs
taken by Heinz von Perckhammer.
Perckhammer. Fuchs. Nice names they have.

And every last airbrushed etc.
We were scared to death.
Thank God he didn't die. Not then.

Eliot's unpublished article,
'On the Physiology of Spanking',
is already writing itself.

Just as the tumescent clitoris
fattens on platelets like a pulse,
so, in the secondary sexual site,

blood and supplementary stimulation
are brought to the epidermis itself.
Rosy-fingered porn. The perfect alibi.

1945: *Learning to Breathe*

Outside, it is raining.
On the road, sparks of rain,
then rain doing a rain dance.

Ski-sticks, deck tennis, quoits
on the pond at Peredelkino.
Through sliding glass,

the garden wavers, bleeds, runs,
a waterfall of falling greens.
Inside, Boris is watching

the way the body breathes.
With difficulty. With concentration.
Totally taken with the task.

The intercostal muscles
manage to part the ribs,
so the rib cage is lifted, up,

for a second, and dropped again.
He sees for the first time
how heavy the weight of it is.

It stirs. The diaphragm tautens,
trembles, and takes the strain,
so the air pressure drops.

To make good the loss,
to right the fault,
air is drawn down the trachea

and into the thorax.
Because Adik is dying at twenty
of his tubercular spine,

he has taught his stepfather this:
that breathing isn't a blessing
but a state of continual crisis.

Instability. Imbalance. Emergency.
Air pressures needing correction.
The rib cage and the heart

are not allowed to rest.
Otherwise he is perfectly still.
Adik lies on the bed like a lizard.

All wiring and spare parts,
on his side, like a kit,
to Borya he is still a little boy,

sent to sanatoria since the age of 11
and getting steadily worse.
Always too busy for Borya,

now he is busy with breathing.
The air is chapping his lips.
Brittle, cracked like a prawn,

but he doesn't complain,
until he suddenly cries out
at the pain in his leg.

Amputated two years ago.
At the top of his thigh,
soapsmooth uncircumcised stump.

Then the buzz of breathing stops.
Adik has seen something
somewhere a long way off.

After the illegal cremation
(Adik's last wish, fixed by Fadeyev),
Zina will bury her first born

under the flowering currant
by the dripping dacha steps
in the harp of the rain.

1946: *Reunion*

Still stencilled with swastikas,
front wheel casings like spats,
peristaltic, single prop,

a Focke-Wulf 190 at Luton
shimmies in the shock of heat,
waiting for Natasha Kroll:

priority flight to Paris,
arranged by Simpson's. Purpose:
fashions for the Christmas windows.

(And meeting her mother,
missed for almost ten years.)
Perfume and petrol

in the cockpit's blister.
The joke of being a Jew
in a German warplane. Laughter.

Petite. A touch of Tartar
in her sloping olive stone eyes.
The mapping pen exactness

of her eyebrows' Indian ink.
Features cleverly asymmetric.
Skin fine as Rizla papers.

She is wearing a Simpson's suit:
five button, neat grey check.
And an overcoat with astrakhan trim,

curly as walnut, slightly waisted,
gold glass rosebud buttons.
Her dark red hat is on her lap

so headphones can be worn
and the pilot proposition her
with dinner, dancing, drinking,

with offers to explain
in detail the etymologies
of jazz and joystick.

Offers she cannot refuse
because her mike-switch is kaput.
Headphones in her lap,

two bakelite bluebottles,
intermittent, indecent, over
and out, she thinks of England:

of hydrangeas in Hyde Park,
subtle shades of litmus,
of helter-skelter whelks at Brighton,

of taking her parents to Lord's,
of a cricket ball in wet outfield
like a circular saw,

of anything English. Novy mir.
Aus der neuen Welt.
And when she holds her mother tight,

the fierce love she feels
exists with irritation. As of old.
Love has broken a rosebud button.

1947: *Novy Mir*

The good offices of *Novy Mir*
and Nina Nikolayevna Yasenkaya
bring out the poet in Pasternak:

a peacock's train of typing keys,
manuscript like mushroom gills,
chandeliers, pewter with dust,

like giant jelly moulds.
An affair with words.
Twenty years between them,

and separated by six feet now:
Borya in Yasenkaya's bed,
wearing jacket, waistcoat, shirt,

tie, vest and woollen underpants,
while the experienced Nina,
widowed twice at 39,

puts a crease in his trousers,
which are sopping wet
from a night on the streets.

He is here to break it off.
Bed preserves his modesty.
8 a.m. She is in her dressing gown.

Unmoved, he sees her body move.
The shift and sway of flesh
he shrinks from. Cold. Old.

On the wireless, the fly duet
from Offenbach. *Orpheus.*
Which she switches off

as her dressing gown opens
and she gets into the bed,
giving him a good long look

at the cleft of her cunt.
Its ragged shadow
complicated like a Yale lock.

Novy mir. Without a hair.
He has only to touch it.
And he has forgotten the cyst

on the side of his skull,
pricked with pores,
disgraceful dandelion head.

Afterwards, he is born again.
She sits on the edge of the bed,
belly a coiled anaconda.

He grins with damp-stained teeth
and pulls off his clothes.
Her last husband, she says,

made love like someone sawing logs.
In out, in out.
The second time, she comes herself,

lost, farting with her cunt,
face turned away,
fist-fucked like a French horn.

1948: *Mystical Delusional Experience*

Rafts, radiators,
pan pipes of icicles,
an organ loft of icicles,

and her son's right leg
perfectly paralysed, too,
tight to the bone

as a descant recorder.
It matches the useless arm
hanging like a broken pointer.

Spring at Winterton Hospital.
The path to Outpatients
and Outpatient Physiotherapy

sunk deep in the snow,
hard, uneven, treacherous,
melted, re-frozen,

like a length of dried snot.
The boy's gabardine shoulders
work as he walks.

Whimpering leather.
The snick of stainless steel.
Bright as sealing wax,

the leg in its caliper.
This rude mechanical,
strenuous, double-jointed.

Like cranking a car.
Effort. Resistance and give.
A rocking horse action.

Completely different
from cases of cerebral palsy,
tottering like marionettes.

Winterton oppresses Olive.
When the fever was critical,
she watched all day,

on tiptoe, calves aching,
through the observation glass
of the isolation ward

for infantile paralysis.
His glazed features
found and lost with fatigue.

Profile clear as a cameo,
then gone. It was two days
before she could turn her head.

Now, behind his spectacles,
the eyes of the physio throb.
A gaze coming and going.

He powders the leg with talc
and lightly rubs: careful
not to tire the little limb.

Or himself. Medical horse manure.
Norman knows he can heal the boy.
By massage with linmethsal.

Features palsied with contempt,
his index finger prods the air,
intimidates the oxygen.

(Like Lenin a long way back.)
His hands conduct his conversation.
He has had all the proof he needs.

(Probably 40% proof, says Eliot.)
Last Sunday, he went back to bed
in his clothes, after his paper round.

And was galvanised. Taken. Possessed.
By Massa, a negro guide.
He said the Lord's Prayer

and called on Massa by name. *Massa.*
Whuff. Norman eyes his audience.
Defies his audience to disagree.

I was big as Battling Siki.
My head hurt from the headboard.
There were weals on my thighs

where the footboard dug in.
I worked the measurements out.
I was six feet seven tall.

Blood on the boil.
An unbearable light.
And afterwards, his neck . . .

(Pain in the neck, says Eliot.
Either a touch of meningitis,
or an epileptic fit

with mild schizoid psychosis.
Thus Eliot Raine MD, FRCP, DPM,
the accredited shrink.)

But the son is cured.
Freddy Gargett an encore.
The left calf muscle grows,

a new development section,
its tone improves,
hardens, relaxes, dynamic

under Norman's virtuoso fingering,
while he sings out of tune
spiritual after negro spiritual.

1949: *Bedlam*

A satisfactory Maudsley morning:
coir-coloured squirrels
flame up the wych elms,

laurel hedges glitter,
the fountain is a firework,
and the star of Bethlehem

(or Bedlam) is focused
in the curve of a Bentley boot,
the long and short of it,

a golden printer's carat.
Morning rounds over,
Eliot settles to Sherlock Holmes:

'The Empty House' and Moriarty,
'motionless as a spider
in the centre of his web'.

When the telephone rings.
The empty warehouse acoustic
announces a butcher who what?

Could you repeat that, please?
Who wants his daughter's kidneys back.
Like chestnuts in pith,

ripped untimely,
for sectioning and preservation.
Bright's. Standard P. M. procedure.

When her body was returned,
he opened it. Professional interest.
To see what the doctors had done.

Eliot can see him, bloodless,
open-mouthed, red-handed,
in his smoking cold room.

Bare window: two packets of Paxo,
a sprig of plastic parsley
on a willow pattern plate,

and a sign saying 'Closed'.
The fume of breath
around his livid lips.

Now he wants her kidneys back,
back in her burgled body.
Eliot: the Napoleon of crime.

Chap in Ward 6 who *was* Napoleon.
Haemorrhoid case from St Mark's,
successively reincarnate,

whose presence is marked
by a light behind his head
whenever he goes to sleep,

and his advent heralded
by signs in the night-time sky.
Celibate scion of God,

and woe to any woman
he should lie with,
damning her to certain death.

God's scientific expertise:
botany, physics, thermodynamics.
Laws at play around His throne.

60. Innocent as his set of dentures.
Except for the sunshine effect
at the head of his bed.

Which disappears instantly
when sister wakes him up.
Staff call him Bright Boy.

Pale blue eyes. Belfast accent.
Forehead furrowed genealogically.
Parting the pitted grey of zinc.

Says everything twice.
Says everything twice.
Hearty double handshake, like Hitler.

This very moment in Garden Square,
Queenie watches her husband Henry,
wearing pyjamas, whistling,

take the cold kettle
and fill a hot water bottle for bed.
Broad daylight. As if she weren't there.

1950: *Missing the Boat*

Zhonya, abandoned in Boulogne,
missing boat after boat
because of that Saturday's storm.

Rain like a cow pissing
and Fedya simply furious.
Her legs wouldn't go up the gangplank.

They counted the luggage,
sat, and set off for the sailing,
but the steamer forced itself

against the granite jetty.
Perverted, hysterical steel.
And Fedya left on his own.

The storm emptied a teapot
the length of the coastline.
Yachts like Hassids in the harbour.

Left to her own devices,
every morning, for a fortnight now,
she cultivates her calm,

drinking coffee in the same café.
Zen. She pays attention to particulars.
The line of drips left on the cup

sometimes makes a book of matches.
Her lipstick sometimes leaves
a segment of blood orange

on her glass of orange juice.
She cares about coincidence,
things coming together.

Her single, solitary once . . .
Beauty behind her at last,
she likes watching the waiter,

a boy with a notch in his nose,
new every morning,
from squeezing a spot.

Now he pulls a palsied face
at the counter's chrome
to corner a pimple

close to his mouth.
Routine eternal recurrence.
As if she weren't there.

So she could stay here forever,
phoning Lydia twice a day,
after every missed sailing.

Meshuggah ist Trumpf,
she shouts into the telephone.
Remember your children, Lydia replies.

Yes. Her children as children,
diving for Mr Husband
down to the foot of the bed:

a warm hot water bottle,
or a cold flabby fool.
Hard to tell the difference. Alas.

Impossible to extricate oneself.
Every rock pool is flypaper
in the lightly falling rain.

1951: *Yam Yar*

Johnnie Frost. Railings webbed,
decorated with dusty nets
like English Italian restaurants.

World gone grey overnight, what?
Distinguished, silver, in sunlight.
Then suddenly drab. Like Wodehouse,

curious cove that Lydia's reading,
where several sentences
of puce Quintilian euphues,

prose of the purest penthouse,
are swiftly succeeded
by a plunge to the basement,

my giddy aunt. (Who heard Hitler,
asked if he spoke French, reply:
vous êtes mon prisonnier. M.G.A.)

Jeeves Takes Charge
is bivouac'd on the kitchen table,
where Jeeves judges Nietzsche

to be 'fundamentally unsound'.
(Odd verdict for a Vichy type.)
Lydia looks as if she's seen a ghost.

Which, in the circs, she has.
Ernst Rosenfeld, wag, Untermensch,
and old Swan vesta from Munich,

who's survived the whole bally show.
Thanks to Ilse, his Aryan wife,
who kept him well hidden.

Not even their kid knew he was there.
For five years. Old Chinese proverb:
the squeaky wheel gets oiled.

Gestapo aiming their oil cans
like churchwarden pipes.
Ghastly. What could a blighter do?

Under the floorboards? Why not?
Rath*er*. Right through the war.
Suited her down to the ground.

High-minded female, my wife.
Kept me out of trouble. O.S.V.s.
Trouble is, she understands me.

A year for his bedsores to heal.
Between suspended floor and ceiling
not a lot of room for movement.

Awake all day in the dark.
No naps. Too dangerous to snore.
Disciplined excretion: nights only,

when no one else could smell.
On a willow pattern plate.
The dread of diarrhoea.

Five years fearing appendicitis;
difficult, though, to catch a cold.
Ration cards for one adult

and one child: food was short
and it was awkward drinking
lying down, hard to tilt.

Warm enough in winter,
but hideously hot in summer.
Toothache only happened once:

worked loose by hand
then twisted out. Painful.
And very tiring for the fingers.

It was like being quadriplegic:
he kept 'clean' with a flannel,
but failed to fall for nurse.

Lisa is sitting on his lap.
Aged six. Hearing a bedspring
of wind. She wants a story read aloud.

To her he is a total stranger,
so she is like his little girl.
Lydia looks. Offended. Tender.

Loving. Frosty. Like his wife.
Lisa is lost in *William*,
his way of saying Yam Yar.

1954: *Case Dismissed*

Alfred Bowes-Lyon, the accused.
Occupation: steel shearer,
on guillotine at Morris Cowley.

Middle-aged, weepy Alf Bowes,
facing the scars on her face,
raised scarlet seams,

sewn like sample cricket balls.
Hit for sixes. And sevens.
But it isn't cricket.

The charge: attempted murder.
Defended by his barrister brother,
the Rt Hon. Thomas Bowes-Lyon.

Exhibit A: the big, blunt axe,
snatched off the coalhouse floor.
Intent, therefore, impossible to prove.

Curved hickory handle,
bell-skirted head, 3 lb weight.
The edge's clean, clipped fingernail.

The defendant was jealous:
she had been to a whist drive.
The assault took place

in the vestibule of Smeddle Street.
The weapon somewhat unwieldy,
the space confined,

constrained by coats,
a murder charge avoided.
Several glancing blows

before the head came off.
The axe, not Mrs Bowes.
(Laughter in court.)

There were no witnesses.
The neighbours at No. 22,
Norman and Olive Raine,

were listening to their wireless set.
Light Programme. Derby Day.
A successful each-way bet

on a 33 to 1 outsider,
the American mount of L. Piggott,
the unfancied Never Say Die.

Neighbours at No. 18
were on holiday at Minehead.
Call Eliot Raine, psychiatrist:

accused is not 'McNaughton mad'.
Clearly, Bowes did not believe
that Mrs Bowes was firewood.

Yet Bowes not legally responsible.
Eliot cites case histories,
frequent family mental trouble:

Nerissa Jane Irene Bowes-Lyon,
confined to Royal Earlswood,
Redhill, Surrey, since 1929.

(There, but not all there.
Alive and kicking and screaming,
though 'd. unm. Feb. 1940',

according to *Burke's Peerage*.
Fenella Bowes-Lyon, the mother,
'failed to fill out forms completely'.)

Related to the Royal Family.
Cousin to the Queen. Tingled web.
Mingled yarn. The case stitched up.

Bowes bound over for 18 months.
And what really happened?
He opened his shoulders.

Olive adjusted the volume
to screen out the screams.
Hysteria for the final furlong.

Opened the battering.
Top edge. Meat of the bat.
Snicks, sweeps, hooks, cuts.

Blood is thicker than water.
Almost as thick as paint.
The lino treacherous as trout,

Dorothy Bowes's cuntstruck face.
Cubist with clefts.
Pitiful prognathous wounds.

There will be scars. In time.
A quilted, muscular collage.
Blue black permanent. In time.

1955: *Radiation Sickness*

When your body is afraid,
as Shura's body is afraid,
it is no use saying

there is nothing to be afraid of.
The body shouts you down:
you have no saliva left,

your elbows and your upper arms
have succumbed to eczema,
granules the colour of Lucozade.

There is a keen, magenta,
in each corner of your mouth,
and confectioner's custard

pale in one tear duct.
Why is he wanted
at the Ministry of War?

His summons is the carbon copy
typed on grey official paper:
dry grass and splinters

frozen in dirty water.
Every letter has its aura,
every stamp its after-image.

Signed with a set of initials,
an indecipherable spider.
Shura has a week to worry,

to wish he had important friends,
and *now*, not Mayakovsky
fifteen million years ago.

The clod in trousers,
out to shock the bourgeoisie.
The crowd in trousers,

acting up the demagogue.
Hard to get him off the phone:
yes, I know your Rolls is waiting,

so I won't be very long;
I'll be five more minutes,
then I'll take questions

for, say, ten minutes more,
then you can toddle off, OK?
Volodya. The myth of Mayakovsky.

A cloud in trousers. Maya.
You never knew where you were.
Whereas now you go to the guichet

at Entrance E and take a ticket.
Which is read by a woman in wellingtons.
You follow her torch

down a set of stone stairs,
along an unlit corridor
to a door with a leather wedge.

A. L. Pasternak? In 1940,
you were posted to the Caspian Sea.
Where you filled in this form.

Shura's handwriting, held
by a corner, as if contaminated.
He has forgotten this form.

Which declares two relatives abroad:
your parents. Leonid and Rosalia.
And Rosalia. Like someone deaf,

Shura mouths the words he hears.
I have two sisters also abroad.
We know you have. We know you have.

Date and initial all corrections.
Towards him, upside-down, the form.
Now you may go. May go.

The pen, comrade. The pen.
In the boulevard's sub-zero dust,
Shura, bloodshot on a broken bench.

The face has gone already.
Only the mouth remains.
Working. Equivocal. In close-up.

A couple are kissing beside him,
the man's hand inside her coat.
A starling's quiet geiger-counter.

1959: *Roniger Dies*

Vell. The Cowley Road Hospital.
Anatomical hands on the blanket.
Chin dipped in desiccated coconut.

Mr Roniger can only say Well,
sister says to Lydia. Vell. Vell.
Here lies the exoskeleton of Roniger.

Brown veins on the back of his hands.
Brown varnished vulcanised gums
like pretzels. Folded fingernails.

(Unfolded fingernails?) He used to say
he was as old as his tongue
and twenty years older than his teeth.

Sheets thin as a ladies' handkerchief.
You can see to the mattress ticking
and outside there is sleet,

a neat layer like tracing paper.
Able to hide less and less.
The thinnest disguises. Vell.

Asked in the past about his past,
he wondered why. Angrily.
Why does anyone want to know?

Source of income: secret.
He could afford to rent the room
and hang about the Union.

One soft leatherette suitcase,
velvet with dust, under the bed
at Garden Square. Not even locked.

Containing pornographic magazines
(*Spick* and *Span* and *Spanking Monthly*)
as well as a letter from Einstein,

in German, and a cornered spider.
Here, on his hospital locker,
a pleated, half-peeled clementine.

Still life. Vell. Last words:
I never liked you when we were alive.
Sleet a Rosetta stone where birds have been.

1960: *False Teeth*

Every flower bed a bed of nails.
Borya's old bath in the nude,
an odalisque holding her pose.

And Yasenkaya kept in the dark,
jealously watching the window
where Borya is dying downstairs,

wedged upright with pillows,
a wax maquette without false teeth.
And serve him right

for Renate, she thinks.
For the way he looked at her,
the way she laughed

with her crinkly nose,
wet teeth, wet eyes. Wet furrow.
Kipper bone of pubic hair.

The way she kept holding his hand,
their interlocked fingers.
Her parted lips. Wet fern.

Yasenkaya can see the television,
Zina's, its four-inch screen
a shiny pellet of chewing gum,

a coathanger's kiss curl,
and Borya's tragic *moue*
more of a coathanger than ever.

A cushion of sunflower seeds
sustains her: a fly's eye,
eaten like embroidery.

She is forbidden the dacha,
politely, by Shura and Zhenya.
So Zina will not be offended?

In case the emotion is too much?
Because they took his teeth away?
His vanity? The reasons change.

(But, were you to ask me,
I'd say she was too demanding.
Marriage. Marriage. And marriage.

Am I wringing or rubbing my hands?
A bit of both. Whetting my wings.
Think of all that foreign currency.)

She waylays Marfa, the nurse,
and discovers they've diagnosed cancer.
Both lungs. Will they operate?

Marfa's hand on her raincoat arm:
when you open up cancer
it blows all over like feathers.

He'll be gone by the morning.
In fact, he is already deceased.
Shura and Zhenya,

brother and son, are busy now
putting letters to death,
letters demanding recognition

and still alive with consequence.
Like hair after death.
Like fingernails. Foreign false teeth.

1966: *Mouth Music*

Spertamozoon worming its way
into his Fauvist left ear,
midwinter maroon,

metal teeth of his cardigan zip
catching the cold afternoon sun,
Jimmy is walking to Padarise

along the Edinburgh–London line,
in his pinstripe suit.
Who does he think he is?

Rasumov? Evelyn Waugh,
ear tundish offered to guests?
Ramusov? Beethoven?

He is making mouth music.
Sometime last month, a shout
came to live in his mouth.

Limping like a skateboarder
because his legs won't stretch
from sleeper to sleeper,

Enid is on his one-track mind.
1915–1955. She Sleeps with the Angels.
Cancer. Black blood in her cunt.

Ened, Hebrew for *delight*.
Iron cliché, the signpost says:
Enidburgh, 120 miles.

Which is where she lives,
in the Garden of Ened.
He pictures it clearly,

a sliver, nothing much,
between two railway lines,
the Gritis and Euphrates:

a pond like mint sauce,
collection plates in the tree,
a hawthorn hedge with crockery.

The turntable a spider's web,
six several lines,
all leading somewhere . . .

His bottom-set stuck out
for comic effect
like a ventriloquist's dummy,

Norman enjoys *Jackanory*,
watching it through binoculars,
when Olive brings in the *Mail*:

Oxford Man Found Wanking
On Edinburgh–London Line.
Our Jimmy. All is forgiven. For now.

Even the fate of Norman's scrapbook.
Whose cover shows two dogs,
torn from scraps of paper,

scrapping. And is empty.
'Fame' filched by Jimmy
for the bar of his pub.

Lost, the only record Norman had.
Posters, cuttings, photographs
of cocky conquests, gumshield out,

ready to be taken by his corner.
Ten years ago? Twelve years ago?
Can I borrow your scrapbook?

Brought it back empty. Posterity.
Now Norman records his voice.
A yard and a half of spools.

Of 'Spanish Eyes'. Of mouth music.
Tone deaf. Not stone deaf.
But Jimmy, not Norman, is nuts.

1971: *Constance*

Zhenya's big black umbrella
weeping from its widow's peaks.
Seed after seed after seed.

Now it stands in a map of grief
next to the plywood door
in this two-room flat

on the outskirts of Moscow.
Zhenya, Alyona, Lisa, Li:
listening, a frieze of elbows

on the tiny kitchen table.
To Nadya. Nadezhda Mandelstam.
Her full mahogany mouth,

the baccy breath,
the henna'd upper lip,
amber stumps in iron settings,

the *café-crème* velvet tongue
harshly pronouncing sentences.
Laying down the law.

Li's doctorate on Shakespeare?
King John is the bard's best play.
Because. The character of Constance:

grief fills the room up
of my something child,
my absent child,

lies in his bed etc., etc.
Recites: then have I reason
to be fond of grief. And nods.

Her second book, the sequel,
is ready in the next-door room.
More dynamite in there.

A new lease of life for M.
She lights another Laika
from the previous stub.

A Dutch fog, she boasts.
What my translator tells.
Because it never clears.

The Pasternaks have brought
an offering of pussy willow,
a big bunch from Peredelkino,

heavy, silky soft, seductive,
like the brush of the sable,
the carnivorous Siberian sable.

She burns the branch-ends.
Lights the gas stove
and thrusts them in the flame.

To make them last.
It is a conscious gesture,
something to be quoted.

She isn't intimate
the way she was ten years ago,
a guest at Peredelkino,

redcurrants from the garden
in her lap, not saying much,
snatching flies,

an old woman in a smock
and dark blue kerchief,
hair in a tidy dumpling,

ten years before,
before the mouth of split mahogany
was broken by words,

the seizure in the grain,
this ripple in her table top
of combed wet hair,

two shades of gold,
her guests bear witness to.
Before this metamorphosis.

1974: *University Challenge*

Drills fzz. Eating a scone,
on the edge of a sofa,
Maria Vladimirovna Romanovna,

heir to the Russian throne,
first cousin of the Queen,
freshman student at LMH,

about to fail prelims
a second time in PPE.
Wrrrugh! The drill cuts out.

We exhaust the weather.
All that blueblooded begetting,
all that DNA, to bring Victoria,

alive, eighteen, and unamused,
to a first-floor rented flat
above a dental partnership.

1977: *Irony International*

A chemical pelt of hoar frost
thick on the garden wall.
The iron gate sticky with cold.

Ectoplasm in every mouth.
Scurf, scales, dandruff, silicates,
minerals, diamonds in Benenson's collar

as he leads the way to the barn
where the bonds have been bagged.
Baler twine like fuses fuming.

A cockerel retches in the rafters,
flares up, tarnishes, fades.
It depends on the light.

Russian railway bonds, tobacco bonds,
North Caspian Oil Exploration.
Worth a million pounds on paper.

Roughly. The rouble equivalent.
They want a tenner to take it away.
A present from Peter's grandfather,

the rascal on the Russian side
who made machines to polish rice
and lost the lot in 1917.

The long drought of history:
dried and broken paint like lichen
all over the St Petersburg palace.

Every year he fucked a ballerina.
The kiss-off was a sapphire brooch.
Fresh feels and partners new.

One of them threw vitriol.
His face looked like that cockerel.
Lost one ear. Rather hot stuff.

Dribs and drabs like Jackson Pollock.
Needed a new quarter-face.
The family still pay her off.

(In 1986, at Sotheby's,
Mussolini's death certificate
will go for £2,640

and Albert Einstein's passport,
the Swiss passport, for £4,180.
James Joyce's death mask

will be withdrawn from sale.)
Across the early morning dusk,
we see a sudden butterfly

tearing itself in two. And again.
These bonds are worthless.
Frozen assets. (Till autumn 1986.)

1982: *History Repeats Itself*

General Eisenhower (all royalties
to the Incorporated Sailors',
Soldiers' and Airmen's Help Society):

London and Abilene,
sisters under the skin.
Swords into ploughshares.

Ike impromptu, on the balcony
of Mansion House, to the crowd:
I am now a Londoner myself.

And JFK to the ditto
at the Brandenburg Gate:
Ich bin ein Berliner.

Norman was vaccinated, she says,
with a gramophone needle.
Here to serve our apprenticeship.

When I came out of the forces,
crocked, if I'd known *then*
what I know *now*, what these hands,

I'd never have put on a boxing glove.
(Swords into ploughshares.)
Out of the forces, crocked.

(I am a zzzzz on the armchair,
dead to the world,
while his healing hands

make a masturbatory click, click,
like a gramophone record come
to its end, its end, its end.)

1984: *Gemäldegalerie, Dahlem*

The electric train am Zoo
like a dead fly on its back:
Craig and Lisa descend

with two Chinese inventors
and their triple-tied luggage:
the acupuncturist is S. J. Wu,

whose business card
gives his adderss in Taiwau;
the puncturist is Jenq Maw Lin Jang,

whose new self-sealing tyre
incorporates a 'casing structrue'
that stops the air from 'leaking ont'.

Two pair caterpillar eyebrow.
Two pair standard tadpole eye.
Good luck. Goodbye. Taiwanese twius.

In the Gemäldegalerie,
Holbein's merchant seals a letter,
his neck silk faintly frayed

and perfectly painted,
goose quill packed with polystyrene.
In the foreground of the Van der Goes,

a single ribbon of straw, creased,
exactly seen and set down
on the canvas: impure gold.

Bruegel's *Blue Mantle* is under glass.
It illustrates proverbial sayings
and was painted 1559, the year

he changed his name from Brueghel.
Where two pair buttocks
loom out from a lean-to loo,

a mass of fingerprints,
exactly seen, set down.
Sie scheissen beide durch dasselbe Loch.

Which means they are close friends.
In *Predigt Johannes des Täufers*,
a woman in the foreground dusk

is caught by Rembrandt
holding her little girl trussed
so she can shit in the river.

Craig pulls the door marked *Drücken*.
Wrong. *Drücken* was the word
that Zhonya used to Fedya,

feeble when he went zum Klo.
And Lisa's passport holds
her father's photograph,

Eliot taken on his deathbed.
Foreshortened face. Eyes shut.
Chin tied tight with a sheet.

Mouth open at each corner
like the symbol for infinity.
Straining to relieve himself.

And the sign for a wheelchair
is exactly like an ampersand.
An ampersand. An ampersand.

Acknowledgements

'The Queen's Own Oxfordshire Hussars', 'NEP and Narkomindel', 'Lenin Takes a Long Bath', 'Berlin am Zoo', 'A Suitcase Full of Shit', 'Asylum', 'Answer the Telephone', '*Du bist wie eine Jude*', 'Mawcarse' and 'Reunion' were first published in *The New Yorker*. My thanks to Chip McGrath, Alice Quinn and Tina Brown.

I am deeply grateful to A. D. Nuttall, Emrys Jones, Michel Treisman, Harvey McGregor, Ann Jefferson, Robin Lane Fox, Jon Stallworthy, Bernard Richards and Bryan Hainsworth. Ben Sonnenberg has been a good friend to *History: The Home Movie*.

READ MORE IN PENGUIN

In every corner of the world, on every subject under the sun, Penguin represents quality and variety – the very best in publishing today.

For complete information about books available from Penguin – including Puffins, Penguin Classics and Arkana – and how to order them, write to us at the appropriate address below. Please note that for copyright reasons the selection of books varies from country to country.

In the United Kingdom: Please write to *Dept. JC, Penguin Books Ltd, FREEPOST, West Drayton, Middlesex UB7 OBR*

If you have any difficulty in obtaining a title, please send your order with the correct money, plus ten per cent for postage and packaging, to *PO Box No. 11, West Drayton, Middlesex UB7 OBR*

In the United States: Please write to *Penguin USA Inc., 375 Hudson Street, New York, NY 10014*

In Canada: Please write to *Penguin Books Canada Ltd, 10 Alcorn Avenue, Suite 300, Toronto, Ontario M4V 3B2*

In Australia: Please write to *Penguin Books Australia Ltd, 487 Maroondah Highway, Ringwood, Victoria 3134*

In New Zealand: Please write to *Penguin Books (NZ) Ltd,182–190 Wairau Road, Private Bag, Takapuna, Auckland 9*

In India: Please write to *Penguin Books India Pvt Ltd, 706 Eros Apartments, 56 Nehru Place, New Delhi 110 019*

In the Netherlands: Please write to *Penguin Books Netherlands B.V., Keizersgracht 231 NL–1016 DV Amsterdam*

In Germany: Please write to *Penguin Books Deutschland GmbH, Friedrichstrasse 10–12, W–6000 Frankfurt/Main 1*

In Spain: Please write to *Penguin Books S. A., C. San Bernardo 117–6° E–28015 Madrid*

In Italy: Please write to *Penguin Italia s.r.l., Via Felice Casati 20, I–20124 Milano*

In France: Please write to *Penguin France S. A., 17 rue Lejeune, F–31000 Toulouse*

In Japan: Please write to *Penguin Books Japan, Ishikiribashi Building, 2–5–4, Suido, Bunkyo-ku, Tokyo 112*

In Greece: Please write to *Penguin Hellas Ltd, Dimocritou 3, GR–106 71 Athens*

In South Africa: Please write to *Longman Penguin Southern Africa (Pty) Ltd, Private Bag X08, Bertsham 2013*

READ MORE IN PENGUIN

A CHOICE OF FICTION

Two Lives William Trevor

'Trevor's adroit playing-off of two worlds in each of the *Two Lives* – the sterile and the sublime – enables him to balance humour and heartbreak in perfect equilibrium' – John Walsh in the *Sunday Times*

A Clockwork Orange Anthony Burgess

'There was me, that is, Alex, and my three droogs, that is Pete, Georgie, and Dim, Dim being really dim, and we sat in the Korova Milkbar making up our rassoodocks what to do with the evening…' Horror farce? Social prophecy? Penetrating study of human choice between good and evil? *A Clockwork Orange* is, dazzlingly, all three.

For Good or Evil Clive Sinclair

'These stories are not only very finely polished but genuinely contemporary, stylistically serious … a striking collection' – *The Times Literary Supplement*. 'Evil, entertaining little fictions … Clive Sinclair is fluent, inventive, linguistically gifted' – Victoria Glendinning in the *Sunday Times*

Spider Patrick McGrath

In *Spider* Patrick McGrath creates a character whose story, told in a storm of beautiful language, slowly reveals itself to be an intricate web of truth and illusion. 'A tale of not-so-ordinary madness which slowly unravels the horrifying enigma at its centre' – Anthony Quinn in the *Tatler*

A Place I've Never Been David Leavitt

'This fine new collection … deftly places the many varieties of love and sexual attraction in perspective, seeing them as part of the vast complex mosaic of human experience' – *The New York Times Book Review*

READ MORE IN PENGUIN

A CHOICE OF FICTION

Summer People Marge Piercy

Every summer the noisy city people migrate to Cape Cod, disrupting the peace of its permanent community. Dinah grits her teeth until the woods are hers again. Willie shrugs and takes on their carpentry jobs. Only Susan envies their glamour and excitement – and her envy swells to obsession... 'A brilliant and demanding novel' – *Cosmopolitan*

A Good Man in Africa William Boyd

'A highly accomplished comic novel, uproariously funny, but also carefully constructed, canny, and artful' – *Observer*. 'A wildly funny novel, rich in witty prose and raucous incidents ... without qualification, a delight' – *Washington Post*

Los Gusanos John Sayles

'Savvy and savage ... a broad and impressive portrait of the last fifty years of Cuban life' – *Washington Post*. 'There is a score of characters in *Los Gusanos* ... each has a story to tell, and Sayles tells them all well ... a vivid read ... exciting, sexy and humorous' – *Independent*

Lantern Slides Edna O'Brien

'Superb ... Her stories unearth the primeval feelings buried just below the surface of nostalgia, using memories to illuminate both what is ridiculous and what is heroic about passion' – David Leavitt in *The New York Times Book Review*

The Woman's Daughter Dermot Bolger

'A novel of enormous ambition, an attempt to create a folk history for those whose dark sexuality has banished them into the underworld of their own country ... a serious and provocative work of fiction' – *Sunday Times*

READ MORE IN PENGUIN

A CHOICE OF FICTION

Father Melancholy's Daughter   Gail Godwin

A young woman's poignant search for self-discovery, *Father Melancholy's Daughter* eloquently exemplifies the struggle within us all to attain grace, inspiration and wisdom in our daily lives. 'Skilfully written, accessible, funny, discriminating, readable and thoughtful' – *The Times Literary Supplement*

The Message to the Planet   Iris Murdoch

'I suspect that when the intellectual map of our own times comes to be sketched out, Iris Murdoch will occupy a position analogous to Tolstoy and Dostoyevsky ... Her vision of the world is heart-rending, but ultimately celebratory' – A. N. Wilson in the *Guardian*

Hemlock and After   Angus Wilson

'He was a very acute observer ... and it was this vigilance, allied to a profound curiosity about the world, that gave his fiction its zest and its social accuracy ... a great novelist' – Rose Tremain in the *Guardian*

July's People   Nadine Gordimer

'So flawlessly written that every one of its events seems chillingly, ominously possible' – *The New York Times Book Review*. 'This is the best novel that Miss Gordimer has ever written' – Alan Paton

The Slave   Isaac Bashevis Singer

The Slave is a powerful drama set against the exotic background of seventeenth-century Poland with all its superstitions, witchcraft and witchhunts, abundant life and appalling prejudices. 'The tale is tragic and warmhearted, full of mellow wisdom learned through suffering' – *Yorkshire Post*